architecture

paramodern architecture
SHUHEI ENDO
edited by Hiroyuki Suzuki

Electaarchitecture

editoral coordination
Giovanna Crespi

page layout
Roberta Leone

translation
Richard Sadleir

editing
Gail Swerling

technical coordination
Paolo Verri
Andrea Panozzo

cover
Tassinari/Vetta

Distributed by Phaidon Press
ISBN 1-904313-43-4
ISBN 978-1-904313-43-4

www.phaidon.com

www.electaweb.it

First published in English 2003
Reprinted in paperback 2006

Printed in Hong Kong

Contents

The Architecture of Shuhei Endo and the Essence of Japan
Hiroyuki Suzuki

Shuhei Endo's steel buildings evoke a sense of freedom in the observer. They express a heightened sense of lightness, almost weightlessness, as this essay will explain, and enshrine a wholly distinctive style.

The choice of materials is the starting point for every form of expression in architecture; the materials reflect the architect's personality and cultural formation. Many architects use the transparency and brightness of glass to create works that are metaphors for our time. Others mainly use reinforced concrete and cement, feeling the all-important point is to express solidity and strength. But Endo clearly favors steel, which, with glass and concrete, is one of the distinctive materials of modern architecture. In this respect, Endo's work might seem to fit the modern tradition. But the way he uses and shapes steel is not a simple repetition of what others have been doing ever since the nineteenth century at least, when cast and wrought iron and steel became common architectural materials, especially after Joseph Paxton built the Crystal Palace. Endo's buildings are unrelated to either of the two stylistic currents associated with the new materials, which we can label neo-classical and neo-gothic. The lightness and expressive freedom typical of his work are unrelated to the established traditions of Western architecture. Take, for example, his work called *Springtecture*, a free-form building made of sheets of corrugated steel. This is a standard material, widely used for lining retaining walls, irrigation canals and tunnels; it is cheap and durable and has rarely been used for specifically architectural purposes. It is hardly suited to the expressive modes of the modern traditions and its use reveals a freedom of choice denied to Western architects.

The modernization of architecture in Asian countries has wavered between attempts to draw on local traditions and attempts to absorb or adapt tendencies that emerged on the international scene. Japanese and Western architecture first made contact after the Meiji Restoration of 1868. (Westerners tend to set the turning point in 1853, when Commodore Perry visited Japan, or 1854, when Japan and the United States signed the Kanagawa Treaty of Peace and Amity.) Western architecture at the time was reviving historical styles; the result in Japan was a period of revivals, and since Japanese architects turned to Britain in the later nineteenth century, they designed many buildings in the Victorian style.

Following the Meiji Restoration of 1868, Japan began to be modernized. When the emperor Meiji moved the capital from Kyoto to Edo and renamed it Tokyo, the Imperial College of Engineering was also founded. Here the students received advanced training in Western building methods; they did not study ways of developing the local tradition through the potential offered by modern technology and materials. The general policy was to transform Japanese towns by adopting Western models and erecting buildings that would achieve this.

When the modern movement spread through the West in the twentieth century, Japan fell under its influence. The works of Le Corbusier and Frank Lloyd Wright were studied no less attentively than Art Nouveau, the Viennese Secession and, later, Expressionism. But, though we can trace the influence of the European avant-gardes and the Modern Movement on Japan and show they had their counterparts here, we cannot conclude that Japan actually had a true avant-garde movement. A true avant-garde can hardly be an imitation of something else; and if the term is relevant to Japan we first have to clarify the difference between the terms "Westernization" and "modernization" (and the historical processes behind them). This could also help us understand how far the attempts to express a specific Japanese identity reveal its cultural independence.

After World War II, one strain in Japanese architecture had affinities with new developments in other countries, while a contrasting tendency sought to retrieve a distinctive national identity. Both approaches used new materials for their strength and durability and adopted original methods of construction. Before the war, architects who were attracted to the new international idiom found they could only evoke these buildings, not replicate them, because they lacked the appropriate construction materials: for example, they were forced to use wood to imitate the specific forms of concrete buildings. After the war, the right materials became available and architects began to think Japan had all the requisites for developing its own avant-garde. At the same time, those architects who were committed to expressing Japan's cultural identity also adopted the new materials, experimenting with steel-frame and concrete structures. The work of Kunio Maekawa, who was deeply interested in work by architects abroad, is significant in this respect. During the fifties, notably in the Kanagawa Prefectural Concert Hall, he largely succeeded in devising a style that both explored the potential of new building techniques and critically reviewed ways to preserve the national identity. As a result of this building and the problems Maekawa solved, a series of achievements established a sort of orthodox modernism. But at the same time, the tensions over the question of the national identity were easing, while the lack of resources in Japan meant that new buildings expressed little more than a certain structural coherence and a character similar in many ways to industrial constructions.

Yet the buildings erected in those years were the basis for subsequent developments in Japanese architecture and led to some important experiments. Of particular relevance to the theme dealt with here were the first attempts at building with corrugated steel. An example was the house Kenji Kawai built for himself in 1957. As an engineer Kawai specialized in designing production facilities and had worked with Kenzo Tange. When it came to his own home his main concern was to design a functional building out of recycled materials. It took the form of an enormous oval tube made out of sheets of corrugated steel. It was set directly on the ground, without foundations or columns, and looked like an outsize *objet trouvé*. The rooms were laid out on two floors. Even today, this strange building remains one of the most radical experiments in contemporary architecture.

About twenty years later, in 1975, Osama Ishiyama, a younger architect, designed a villa called *Gen-an*. Ishiyama had been greatly struck by Kawai's house and *Gen-an* was conceived as a response to the impression it made. *Gen-an* was likewise a tube with a corrugated-steel envelope, but unlike Kawai's house its section was triangular, not oval. Another distinctive feature was that at each end there was an independent element, also made of corrugated steel, linked to the main block. Kenji Kawai had produced an experimental building but Ishiyama's can be called an avant-garde work.

Kawai and Ishiyama established a tradition in Japan, showing how corrugated sheet steel could be used in architecture. They converted a civil-engineering material into a building material and opened up new possibilities in architecture.

This leads us to ask just how Shuhei Endo, who belongs to an even later generation, came to use corrugated steel, the hallmark of his architecture. Early in his career, Endo designed a factory. This is a characteristic theme of modern architecture, the relationship between industry and architecture, evident in the work of many architects—Peter Behrens, for example. The experience must have given him an insight into the potential, both formal and expressive, offered by industrial materials. He drew on these qualities with characteristic freedom, a quality that distinguishes his work from that of his predecessors.

Materials similar to those that Endo has insistently experimented with are commonly used by architects for qualities such as strength and economic convenience. In the twentieth century, industrial materials were used in certain societies to show that industry was an important part of their identity, and Endo's choices were actuated by similar motives. But the distinctive feature of his buildings, with their limited range of materials, is their

Kenji Kawai, Kawai
House, Toyohashi,
1957.

Osama Ishiyama,
"Gen-an" House,
Aichi-ken, 1975.

permeability, their generous openings, and their "skin." The very names of his works, *Skintecture*, *Springtecture*, *Rooftecture*, are evidence of his approach. He stretches a sheltering "skin" over buildings with unconventional configurations to protect their ordered but open spaces.

The use of steel in modern architecture is largely bound up with the expressive modes of Western architecture; but Endo's works are unrelated to this history. He uses steel with a freedom that has cut its ties with all tradition. He sees his buildings not as ways of defining spaces but of covering places, sheltering them, without enclosing them in an envelope. In his buildings, corrugated steel sheets are handled in ways that alter their essentially functional and instrumental nature: they curl like strips of apple peel, they cluster round a structure in overlapping layers like petals, they are arranged on different levels to form continuous membranes, and they create fluid spaces with a lightness that is the distinctive quality of each building.

Endo's works have a twofold character. His materials usually evoke the world of industrial production, from which they are directly taken, but the way he shapes them creates a close and intimate relationship with nature, so that the buildings seem to blend into their settings. This means that his buildings should not be seen as celebrations of industry or industrial civilization but as attempts to confer an identity on open spaces in the undifferentiated space of contemporary life.

As for the key idea of "openness," which Endo plays on in various ways, we need to examine it more closely. Traditional architecture in Japan is essentially a series of open spaces: groups of mostly one-story buildings and gardens are arranged in patterns like the tiles of a mosaic. Traditional Japanese buildings are inseparable from gardens. The main rooms are always laid out so they open onto gardens and their spaces are extended into courtyards, as part of a conception that sees no value in enclosed, isolated spaces. If we return to this tradition we can understand where the originality of his buildings stems from, the origin of the singularity of the agenda he is pursuing, as he twists the "skin" of his buildings, using sheet steel in rolled layers to define volumes that are never fully enclosed. Spaces are cut out inside these membranes; their arrangement is free from the constraints entailed by the traditional structure of horizontals and verticals.

His approach is similar to that adopted by the fashion designer Issey Miyake: Miyake also creates a dress from a single sheet of cloth. Instead of sewing a dress as a set of three-dimensional parts, Miyake, inspired by the tradition of the kimono, drapes and folds a single sheet of fabric into a dress. In much the same way, Endo shapes sheets of steel into the highly original forms of his buildings.

The globalized world is awash with buildings that are anonymous because they are "universal," adaptable, undifferentiated. For this reason, many of the attempts to foster a distinctive quality of architecture and assert its individuality have produced anachronistic results. A need of our time is to combine the universal and the individual: this is what Endo's architecture sets out to achieve.

Paramodern Architecture
Shuhei Endo

In these pages, I use the term "Paramodern" to indicate a set of possibilities that modern architecture has never explored, though they are implicit in the various experiments usually covered by the term "modern." These are opportunities not taken, but they have nothing to do with specific forms and styles. The modern, the typical and dominant expression of the West, has taken reductionist thinking to an extreme; it achieves its characteristic expression in abstract, highly reproducible spaces. But this approach has also led to the progressive obliteration of meanings, so that richness and diversity have been lost.

It used to be thought that every construct produced a concordance between sign and significance through metaphor. But in more recent times this conviction has been undermined by the post-modern enterprise, which confronts not meanings but signs and is driven not by the need for communication but self-assertion, while it neglects the content of communication itself. This meant that study of the space-time nexus has given way to experiments aimed solely at the continual manipulation of indeterminately variable signs, which reflect the historical styles.

An antidote to postmodernism might, perhaps, have been found in Metabolism, a movement that explored the processes by which forms are generated. Based on evolutionary assumptions, Metabolism questioned the idea that architecture is the expression of unchanging principles, seeing it rather as the definition of recognizable forms. The structures actually designed by the Metabolists expressed this faith in the power of generative form as a reaction against the principles of symmetry and standardization. However their work betrayed both technical shortcomings, caused by the small number of structural variables they worked with, and formal weaknesses that stemmed from the narrowness of their spatial vision.

At present architecture seems to have settled either for the arbitrary manipulation of striking forms, in the hope of creating a sensation, or an esthetic of asceticism squeezed out of minimalism. Examined closely, the first of these is a game played on the computer; the second is a magical vanishing trick that eliminates meaning. But "significance" in architecture is synonymous with space and time, spatial and temporal contexts that are meant to be understood and shared. Anyone who, like me, has experienced the violence of exclusion, will naturally resist every form of elimination and exclusion. If we think and work in terms of sharing we have to reject exclusion of the kind produced in architecture by geometrical designs that are immutable in space and time, or the reduction of three-dimensional forms to black and white surfaces—in short the expressive modes of minimalism. This

Cursive "Renmentai,"
a style of calligraphy
with the brush
common in Japan
and China.
A "Kanji" character
inherited from
the Chinese tradition
of calligraphy.

approach is essentially a desire to exclude everything not immediately reducible to strict Cartesian spaces. The uniformity that is typical of this esthetic, which separates and isolates, contains the germs of an attitude that seeks to eradicate differences.

In making this criticism, I do not mean to reject the legacy of the modern, which provides the underpinning of minimalism. The problem is not modernity as such; it is the excessively selective attitude towards its great potential that is responsible for the narrowness of the modern movement's later development.

The tendency to abstraction in modernism has grown out of its attack on significance. It is also a result of the conviction that, on a planetary scale, communication is one-way and one-dimensional. But a culture is a chain of specific meanings created in historical time and space. Recognizing the shared values underlying these specific meanings entails grasping diversity. Today, however, there is a marked tendency to understand and share only a restricted time and space, whereas an awareness of belonging to different cultures ought to mean appreciating the different values they embody as a way of sharing their rich diversity.

These are the roots of the repression that leads to abstraction, the rejection of otherness, which leads us to turn away from the labyrinth of languages.

In architecture, one of the effects of abstraction is to neutralize the colors of spaces, a result of rejecting semiotics applied to light, color and form. By doing this, perhaps out of a desire to avoid designs that evoke exclusion, architects end up conceiving spaces that respond solely to the rules of geometrical reductionism. This creates a form of abstraction that, despite its apparent neutrality, conceals a form of coercion: the elimination of differences. Pure white and plain geometrical forms are no guarantee against exclusion. We need to explore different approaches and use other methods if we are to realize modernism's neglected potential.

Modernism codified the value of reproducibility: to make something of it, we need to rethink the gap between abstraction and meaning and reconsider our methods, starting from those offered by geometrical reductionism. Any artifact, any construct, can be reproduced, if it has been fashioned by reductionism. But what has been subjected to reductionism may also be reconstructed so as to acquire a different degree of reproducibility in its new life. Of course artifacts vary in their degree of reproducibility, in inverse proportion to their degree of finish, and today this rigidity determines their value. Though every construct has a role in defining the ways a spatial pattern is perceived, at present it is weak constructs,

Shinto temple of Ise. View of the complex from above. The temple is rebuilt every twenty years. Domestic altar ("Kamidana") dedicated to the transcendental deities of the Japanese religious tradition.

susceptible to transformation, that appear most appropriate. Rigid, unchangeable spaces cannot respond to changing circumstances; they merely simulate a stable organization of the parts of which they are composed; in reality they are made up of undifferentiated elements that can be used for continually changing simulations.

Today we share a common geometric paradigm and live in the midst of the standardization produced by widely available information technology, and we have equal access to all kinds of information. But humanity has not changed; each of us is different, each of us belongs to a specific space-time environment.

I use the term "paramodern" to describe my own approach to architecture (without meaning to suggest a higher value than I would attribute to modernism). It is intended to define the character of the spaces I design, with reference to the Japanese context and the buildings presented in this book, using common architectural methods common to capture their essential qualities.

To clarify the terms "paramodern" and "weak constructs," I shall take an example from my own culture, namely Japanese script. Take the character of the cursive script known as *Renmentai*. This term indicates a style of calligraphy that is common in Japan and China. In *Renmentai* the brush is never lifted from the sheet of paper and all the lines forming the characters are continuous. Moreover there are no gaps between the characters, so that the text forms an unbroken pattern. Cursive styles are not unique to Japan; they are also found in Arabic and Latin scripts. But continuous cursive scripts, in which the separate words are run together, are a distinctive feature of cultures where the brush is used for writing. Furthermore the brush offers considerable freedom in forming the letters; the amount of ink used in making the strokes can be varied greatly. In short, the brush is a weak instrument for determining the form of the strokes: each character possesses the forms received from the free gestures of the calligrapher. The result is to eliminate the differences between the strokes in Chinese characters (*Kanji*), effacing the essential difference between radicals and phonetics, which indicate meaning and pronunciation. The script becomes a continuous whole, weakly constructed, which cannot be broken down into its separate parts: it is formed by the sharing or "partial sharing" (*Bunyu*) of its parts.

Now, returning to my practice as an architect, perhaps it is easier to explain the aim expressed by the concept of "partial sharing" by using the term *Renmentai* to indicate spatial configurations defined by continuous lines. These lines do not correspond to structural parts such as loft, wall or roof: they are continuous and undifferentiated strips of material.

Traditional Japanese architecture is based on a standardization of the features and parts of each room. Spaces separated by sliding doors can merge to form a continuous space when the doors are removed. The spaces are intrinsically "weak." An arrangement of this kind lends itself to continual manipulation, which can alter the structure of the complex and modify its spatial continuity. An example of this is the Katsura Detached Palace.

Another way of defining a spatial hierarchy is to transform spaces by using folding screens or other equally "weak" elements of separation. Moving a folding screen changes the significance and the hierarchical layout of a space, but its value—a flexible continuity—remains unchanged. This idea of a variable continuum is a "weak construct." It may lead to a non-reductive way of thinking about architecture. Moreover, the forms of manipulation I have described amount to abstract acts, which produce a systematic organization of signs.

The weak constructs we see in cursive (*Renmentai*) calligraphy are made possible by the fact that the different strokes that make up the characters are run together. This is analogous to the mutable, flexible and "weak" spaces in traditional Japanese buildings. The rooms are separated by sliding doors, both front and back of a continuous space. In this case, too, the sharing (*Bunyu*) takes the form of a "sharing of parts" with an approach that rejects reductionism.

"Sharing by parts," "partial sharing": these terms express the essential meaning of "symbiosis," the living by sharing found in the natural world. They also mean a shared destiny: destruction of one of the organisms in the community means the destruction of

Katsura Detached Palace, Kyoto. Continuity of space achieved by sliding doors.
In traditional Japanese houses, the use of folding screens "Byobu" makes for a flexible division of spaces.

The automatic distributors and convenience stores on street corners of Japanese cities.

the other. The closeness of symbiosis reflects the impact that our every act has on the world. But the different ways in which each part accepts the primacy of sharing in the relationship can vary greatly and are charged with potential.

The decisive factor in conceiving architecture in Japan is awareness of the limited space of life compared with that of transcendence, i.e. of the other in itself, of the abstract whole, where different deities exist on a single plane and are therefore interchangeable. The characteristics of these divinities, however, are independent of space and time; their attributes are associated with geography and the weather, with the passing of the seasons, the flowing of rivers, the movement of the sea, the forms of mountains. Then these transcendental beings are found everywhere all the time. You find altars to them even in factories or on construction sites, and their worship influences everyday life.

This outlook is illustrated by a distinctively Japanese ceremony: the periodic rebuilding of the Ise Shrine. Every twenty years, the Inner Shrine, in which the deity resides, is ritually moved. The deity, having no material form, exists only in our consciousness; it is independent of place and does not always inhabit the temple, which is only the place where it can be invoked. This amounts to setting the same value on void and substance, with an awareness that the two parts of a thing form a single shared whole, like inside and outside, right and wrong.

There are even more prosaic examples of this outlook. The vending machines so common in Japanese cities are one of the ways people come into contact with "partial sharing" or "sharing by parts." The example is apt not just because a vending machine can

Model for
Springtecture S,
competition design
for a ferry terminal,
Sasebo, Nagasaki,
2000–01.
Model for
Springtecture H,
pavilion with toilets,
Shingu-cho, Hyogo
1997–98.

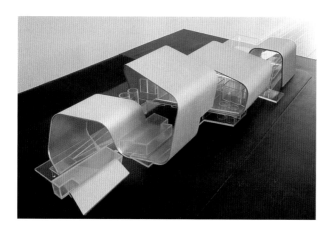
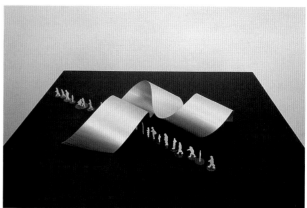

contain different kinds of drinks, so confirming the importance of interchangeability: the interchangeability of the drinks it offers enables the machine to satisfy a desire, not just meet a need. The same principle applies to a convenience store, a form of shop modeled by the desires of is customers; it can even explain the spread of cellphones. In each case we find the common tendency to pack different functions into a single "weak construct" that communicates by transforming itself.

Japanese culture is the fruit of a way of thinking characterized by permeability, in some ways analogous with the tendency toward abstraction in the modern West. It also grows out of sharing through the abstraction of significance, as shown by the separation of form from meaning in the Japanese language and Japanese writing. The former results from the reading of the latter, which in turn is based on the use of Chinese characters, pronounced in the Chinese way, and in this form incorporated into the language.

For these reasons, my "paramodern" architecture is based on *Renzokutai* structures: continuous surfaces or strips that form the outer shell, floors and roofing, in their continuity partly sharing (and shaping) the complete building they define. These strips shape weak "constructs" or "artifacts," and within the spaces they define they do not generate differences because no single element dominates the others. Partial sharing means there are no boundaries between the parts, nor symmetries of point and line, since a continuously generative form never achieves a settled configuration. Symmetry expresses an a priori approach, a simulation produced by viewing the object from the outside. But the architecture of continuous forms, *Renmentai*, rejects the authority of a priori forms and seeks the endlessly mutable and the indeterminate.

Starting from these concepts, my buildings are experiments in the use of strips of corrugated sheet steel. Of course this is not the only possible material; concrete or steel panels could be used in much the same way. I chose corrugated steel solely for technical and economic reasons.

Strips of steel can be used to separate interior and exterior by exploiting their linear and surface continuity, by simply folding them so they match the measurements required and suit the features of the site. To distribute the loads and stresses uniformly, the sheet steel has to be folded to form continuous curves or continuous sequences of planes and curves. The interiors can be divided up by bolting the sheets together so their curves produce continual inversions of open and closed, of interior and exterior, diversifying the spaces and integrating them at the same time, giving them the qualities of a new abstraction.

In modernism, architects divide interiors into pillars and beams, roof and walls, and then assemble them. This method of "assembling" buildings is one of the principal limitations of modern architecture. My experiments start by questioning the two fundamental "principles" that underlie this approach to architecture: the separation of interior and exterior and its division into components such as pillars, infill panels, facing materials, party walls, and so forth. So my idea of paramodern architecture is embodied in two kinds of constructions. I call the first kind, mainly consisting of open spaces, *Halftecture*. The second kind, in which walls and roofs are replaced by continuous ribbons of sheet steel, I call *Rooftecture*.

works and projects

Cyclestation M
bicycle deposit
Maihara-cho, Shiga 1993–94

This simple structure is a bicycle deposit. The building stands on the square in front of the west exit from Maibara Station on the Shinkansen Line, about 40 minutes from Osaka. Planned for a small, city-owned parcel of land on the square, this facility itself cannot accommodate all the bicycles usually left in the square. The brief was to design a building that would enhance the urban landscape. Many train stations in Japan urgently need bicycle deposits. Construction of these facilities is generally not so much part of a coherent plan as a response to one of the unsightly side-effects of the large numbers of people that use railway stations. Essentially it was a way to deal with the eyesore created by abandoned bicycles.

Bicycle deposits tend to be enclosed because the main concern is security.

The design of this building sought to achieve openness and clearly identify a place where bicycles could be left. It was hoped this would make the building easily recognizable and so prompt more people to use it.

The building is perfectly simple in composition, with car parking and accommodation for the custodians on both levels. The upper level has a horizontal floor with access by a curved ramp. A slightly off-vertical spiral staircase linked to a footbridge leads down to the square. The roof is made of corrugated steel: it continues the convex wall of the façade to form a continuous, seamless structure: in its simplicity it defines a broad open volume. The design explores ways to create architecture that serves an urban function without being closed to the outside.

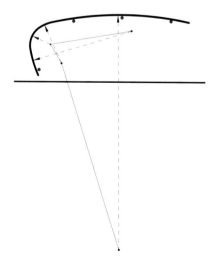

Elevations facing the square and station.

Plans of first and second floors and of west
and north elevations.
Views of interior and exterior of entrance side.

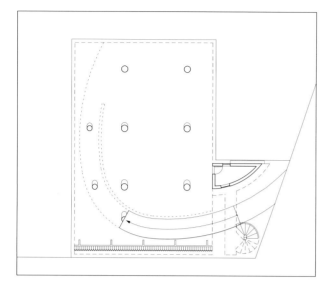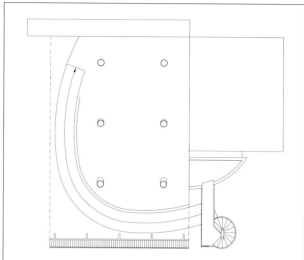

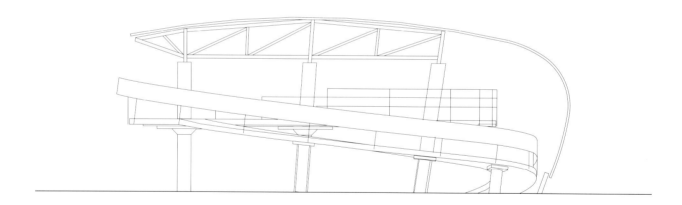

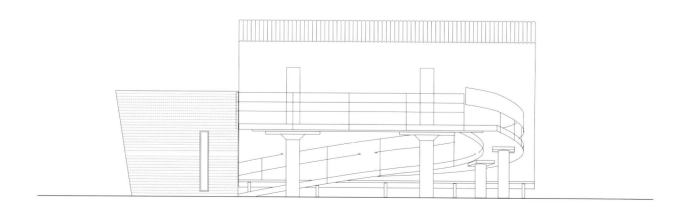

Healtecture K
home-clinic
Takatsuki, Osaka, 1994–96

This house, located in a suburb of Osaka City, is the home of two generations of a family. It is also the client's workplace: formerly a researcher at a well-known pharmaceutical company, here he engages in healing activities for the local community as his second career.

Though this is a densely built-up residential area, the client's brief was that the architecture should create openness in a wide range of relationships, an obvious necessity for the family-run clinic on the first floor. Apart from this, the need to create a relationship with the outside (in a form expressing outreach) stemmed from a new conception of medical practice, inspired by the client's wish to emphasize the relatedness of all living beings, as in the circulating equilibrium of all bodily energies.

Openness was an essential part of the client's approach to healing. The holder of a doctorate in pharmacology, his first involvement in healing came through Oriental medicine. To restore the smooth energy flow in the body by removing stagnation or obstruction, he believed it was essential for his patients to maintain a non-exclusive state, receptive to external stimuli. For this purpose, an open system is always advisable and this means creating specific connections.

In response to his client's philosophy, Endo sought to achieve a fully open design. The main façade is glass, which opens up the field of vision and is permeable to light and air. One side is faced with two parallel strips of corrugated steel, modeled with varying degrees of curvature. One of them rises perpendicularly, the other obliquely from the ground: they form the roof and then come to an end at the top of the wall on the opposite side. Slits formed by the intersection of the two surfaces project a complex pattern of light down to the entrance level.

The layout of the building is simple: the steel envelope is attached to a rigid steel frame. The first floor is divided into a pharmacy for Chinese medicines and a clinic for acupuncture and moxibustion therapy. It also contains an open-space hallway. On the second floor and above, there are two split-level home units set on the east-west axis, with access provided by two separate spiral staircases in the middle. The entrances to these units share an intermediate landing, from which the two staircases, winding in opposite directions, lead to the floor above. These become inside staircases at the entrance on the third floor.

Each unit has a large room, with the functional LDK core of the apartment, plus a number of private rooms. The large rooms open to the south like vestibules, widening the field of vision and letting in air and light. The fourth floor is the attic: the curve of the roof and the rigidity of the sheet steel make supporting beams unnecessary.

The difference in level and the narrow cavity between the two sheets of steel enable each unit to be given a small terrace outside and improve the exposition, view and ventilation of the rooms on the building's north front. Glazed screens cover the upper part of the huge open-plan space inside, one set flush with the façade and another set back from it, forming a double translucent layer facing south. This creates a perceptual and spatial continuity between the interior and the exterior and, vertically, between the first two levels of the building.

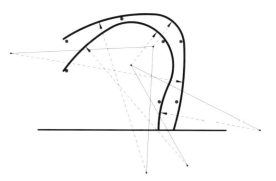

View and detail of the urban front of the house.

Plans of first and second floors and longitudinal sections. Key: 1 preparation of medicines 2 surgery 3 doctor's office 4 pharmacy 5 waiting room 6 living room of the lower apartment. Elevation on the street.

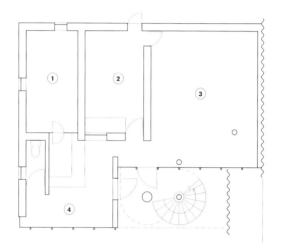

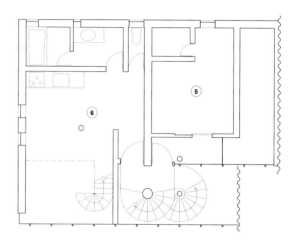

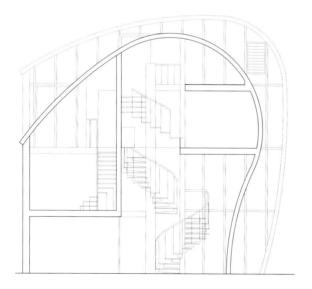

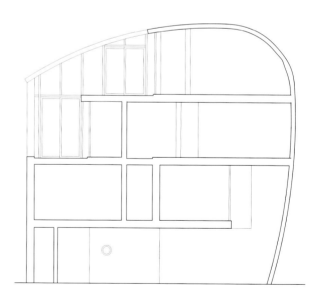

Details of the internal staircase of an apartment and the exit to the roof terrace.
Superimposition of the curved roofs in the attic story.

Please delete address not required before mailing

PHAIDON PRESS INC.

180 Varick Street

New York

NY 10014

PHAIDON PRESS LIMITED

Regent's Wharf

All Saints Street

London N1 9PA

Return address for USA and Canada only

*Return address for UK and countries
outside the USA and Canada only*

Dear Reader, Books by Phaidon are recognised world-wide for their beauty, scholarship and elegance. We invite you to return this card with your name and e-mail address so that we can keep you informed of our new publications, special offers and events. Alternatively, visit us at **www.phaidon.com** to see our entire list of books, videos and stationery. Register on-line to be included on our regular e-newsletters.

Subjects in which I have a special interest

☐ Art   ☐ Contemporary Art   ☐ Architecture   ☐ Design   ☐ Photography

☐ Music   ☐ Art Videos   ☐ Fashion   ☐ Decorative Arts   ☐ *Please send me a complimentary catalogue*

Mr/Miss/Ms   Initial   Surname

Name

No./Street

City

Post code/Zip code   Country

E-mail

This is not an order form. To order please contact Customer Services at the appropriate address overleaf.

Transstreet Geba
park and playground
Fukui, 1994–96

The design for this 2.5 hectare park includes open lawns with a hill laid out as a playground to the west and a concrete structure forming a pedestrian path and a terraced artificial waterfall to the east. The path, about 120 meters long, rises from ground level to a maximum height of 2.5 meters before returning to ground level again. Sections of wall are arranged irregularly to leave gaps on either side of the path. The visitor walking between the curved segments of wall has a transfigured visual perception of the relations between interior and exterior. While the wall passes through various transformations in plan and elevation, the slope has the geometrical rigor of a sequence of arcs. At the top of the path, the visitor sees the waterfall opening out to the west with terraces set at 90° and 45° angles. Gravity causes the water to fall naturally and fan out along different lines of flow to a shallow pool below. On the eastern side a grassy hillock retains a formal relationship with the cascade through the irregular steps set against the wall.

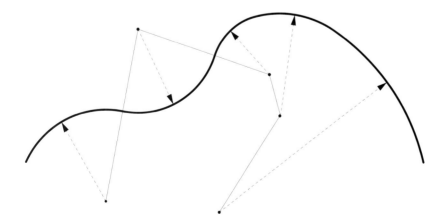

The ramp for pedestrians seen from the north.

West, north, south, and east elevations of the ramp
with the fountain and the general plan of the park.

The footpath seen from the south-east and detail
of an arched underpass.

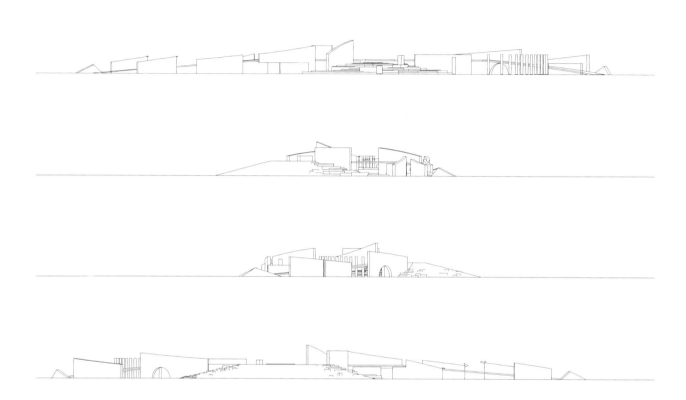

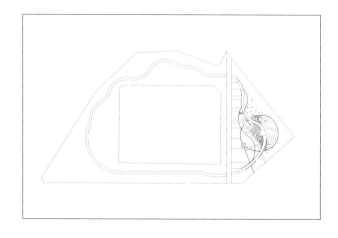

Skintecture I
fish research center
Singu-cho, Hyogo, 1994–96

This research center, about one hour by train from Osaka on the Shinkansen Line, belongs to the Ibogawa Fishery Cooperative, which manages the Ibo River that flows through the area. Despite its largely natural setting there is a concrete plant nearby, so the whole front elevation on the road had to be closed off. For this purpose a new, expressive architectural design was devised. The 60 mm thick cladding of corrugated sheet steel is an excellent insulating material. It offers sufficient structural strength to withstand wind pressure, while its flexibility allows it to be modeled freely. The façades are shaped into irregularly curving bands set on columns spaced at short intervals that follow the triangular shape of the site. The uprights intersect the plane of the second and third floors, creating a grid that underpins the layout of the interiors.

The laboratory conducts research into the dynamics of moving water, with practical spin-offs. Most of its studies involve observation of the surface movement of the water, with results that prompt further research. The water in the hatchery pool ripples to and fro, attracting the viewer's fascinated gaze.

In designing the building, the architect sought to capitalize on the relationship between the two. A fluid sequence of curved and linear surfaces forms the outer walls of the building. The first and second floors are markedly asymmetrical in plan. In the stillness of the architectural object these discontinuous walls produce an effect similar to the ripples moving across the water: they fascinate the viewer and rivet his attention. The aim here is to arouse the observer's interest by the elusive quality of the outer wall, using movement to lure him into fuller engagement.

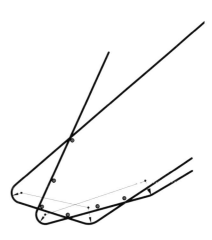

View and reverse angle of the elevation facing the roadway.

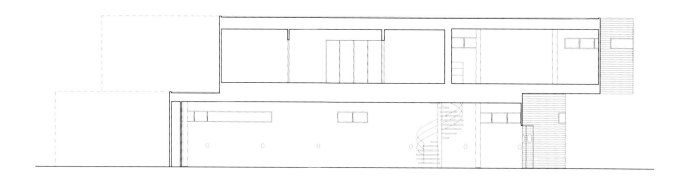

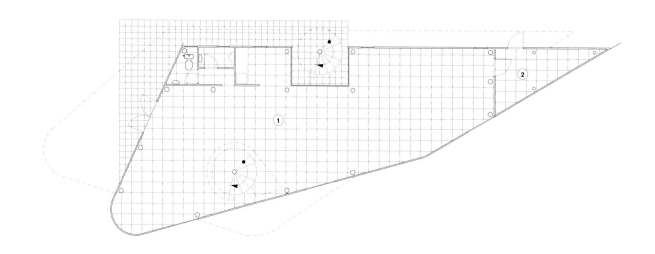

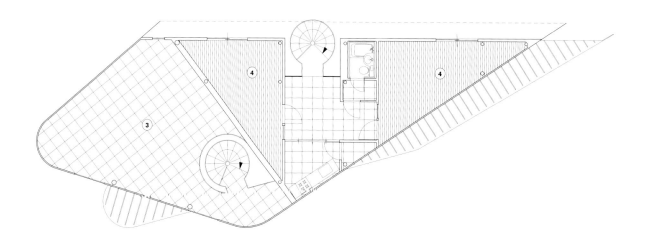

Longitudinal section
and plans of first
and second floors.
Key: 1 laboratory
2 storehouse
3 conference room
4 common room.

Staggered volumes
at the south end of the
building and a view
from above of the
laboratory in its natural
setting.

Transtation O
station shelter
Sakai-cho, Fukui, 1995–97

The function of an unmanned train station may seem to need no description. In this case, however, the aim was to encourage the locals to socialize by providing additional facilities. The narrow site the station occupies used to be a siding, running parallel with the track. To the east there is a small group of houses, on the west extensive rice fields. Over the next few years it is planned to replace the fields with new housing to create an area with a more urban character. Though this may not generate any significant increase in passenger traffic, the station is sure to play an important part in the community's life.

The new station includes parking areas for cars and bicycles and spaces for waiting passengers. Because of the shape of the site, a long corridor had to be incorporated into the architecture. This took the form of a permeable open gallery with easy access at many points. The building is a continuous structure made of sheets of corrugated steel. Since this area gets frequent snowfalls in winter, heavy-duty steel was used in thicknesses from 2.7 to 7 mm, as required. Corrugated steel is flexible and easy to shape into a variety of forms; three structures with different sections were used here. One was a simple cantilever shelter with one end anchored to the ground. In the second type, the cantilever was completed by a frame with regular perforations in it. In the third both sides of the sheet-metal arch rest on the ground. One or other of the three types was used, depending on the required degree of openness to the context, but there is no great difference perceptible in the whole. Galvanized steel was used for greater durability. Ground lights are recessed in the paving of the platform: they provide attractive nighttime illumination with their beams reflected off the underside of the steel vaults.

To make the station a point of social focus for the community it was designed as a continuous structure with roofs and walls forming a single envelope and, above all, with no marked break between interior and exterior.

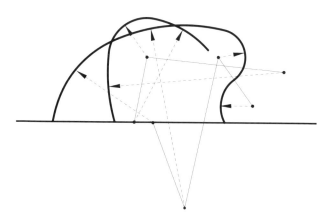

Interior of the sequence of corrugated steel arches with a variable section seen by night and by day.

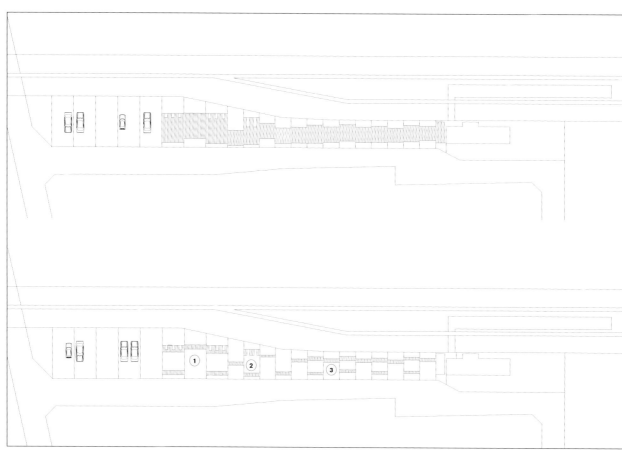

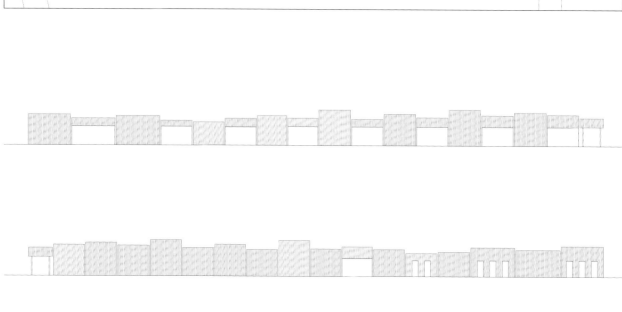

Plans of the roofs of the platform and west and east elevations. Key: 1 bicycle deposit 2 station shelter 3 arcade.
The shelter set parallel to the tracks and detail of the west front.

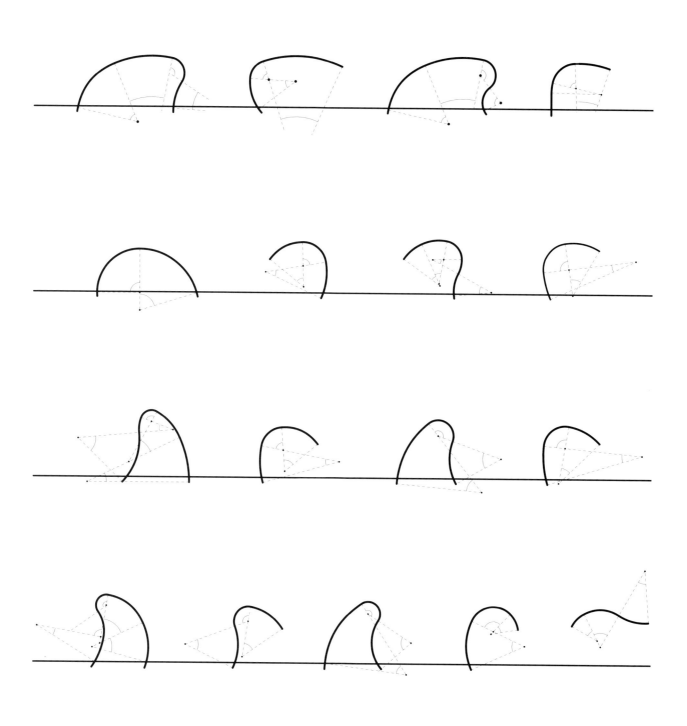

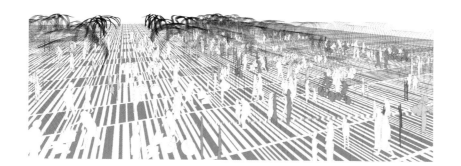

Diagram of the sections and computer concept
of the project.
Details of the structure.

45

Halftecture F
station shelter
Fukui, 1996–97

This small unmanned station consists of a single platform where passengers wait for trains. Local private railways, faced with declining passenger numbers, cannot afford to keep up their existing stations, let alone build new ones. However, the planned construction of a large public facility nearby meant that a new station was needed. The decision to build it was taken despite the fact that local residents, living in the open countryside, rely heavily on automobiles. The railroad is mainly used by older people and children.

The site was not originally earmarked for a new station. The small piece of land needed to build the station was carved out next to the tracks. Only a platform and two sheltered waiting areas were built. Since this is a single track railroad and the driver has to manage the whole operation, the two waiting areas had to be placed at the two points where passengers board trains headed in one or other direction. The material used was corrugated steel modeled into a continuous form. Since the area gets heavy snowfalls, a double layer of sheet steel was used for greater strength.

Most of the steel parts were galvanized to reduce maintenance. Strictly speaking, the station has no indoor spaces. The basic idea is that the design can be expanded by the continuity between the shelters and the platform as an artificial ground-level. An unmanned station might seem simpler than just about any other building; however, as shown by the relation between the two waiting areas and the platform, it is a unique space that combines stasis and movement.

A station is essentially a point of transit; its quality can be enhanced if it favors contacts. But architecture is meant to be more than a point of transit, it is meant to induce people to linger and meet. So this unmanned station can only be described as "half architecture" or Halftecture, built for people in transit and, at the same time, to foster socialization: a little experiment in human contact.

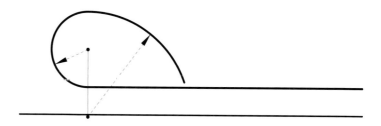

Shelter at the north end and view of the east front.

Plan of the platform, east elevation and sections.
Key: 1 platform 2 shelters.
Elevation of the structure seen across the tracks.

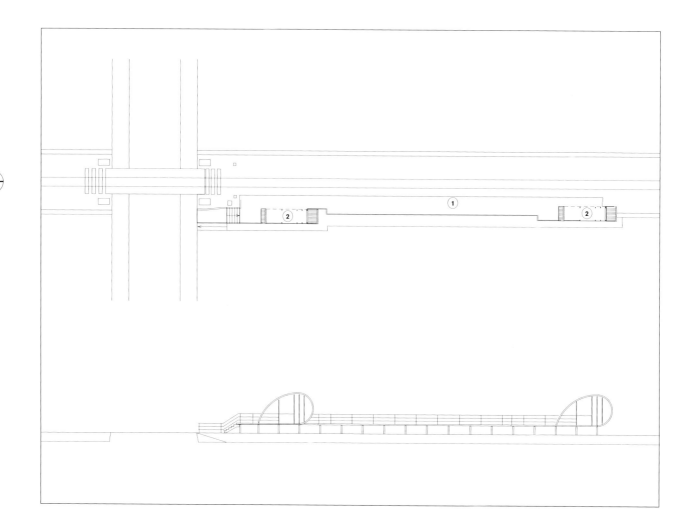

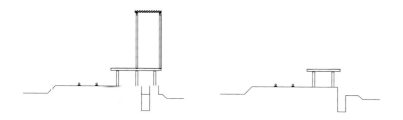

Rooftecture T
square with facilities
Fukui, 1996–97

The site is a suburb about three hours by car from Osaka. It was originally city-owned pasture-land visited by both adults and children in the arc of the day. Its closeness to housing meant that it combined an urban function with a more local character.

The brief was to give the place a formal, public guise and to make use of the relatively pure water from a nearby irrigation canal. The main feature of the project is a water garden surrounded by a flat L-shaped concrete shelter facing the road to the south. A circular skylight pierces the roof at the junction between the two arms of the L. The building is comparatively low in the area by the entrance porch. On the western side an independent brick wall provides a screen against the rays of the afternoon sun. A slender horizontal slit between the wall and the roof slab avoids any sense of oppression and emphasizes the long wooden bench, with a circular cross-section, running along the base of the wall. Set at right angles to the entrance porch is a terrace placed two steps lower running along the roadway on the south, beyond the water garden. Behind this, on the south side, is a patio paved with a local siliceous stone. Completing the layout on the northern side is an artificial embankment 2 meters high covered with grass. On the L-shaped corner there is a multi-purpose area with closed service rooms. Breaching the rule that the pillars should be arranged to form a regular, rational pattern, the distinctive feature of this architecture is the irregularity of the supports, which are clustered in little groups to create a differentiated space. Though the uprights do not all carry the same weights their arrangement is not arbitrary but proportioned to the load surfaces. In addition to preserving the memory of the originally undivided piece of land, this arrangement also creates a recreational area that fosters contact between the visitors.

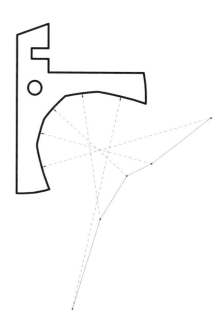

The water garden and the entrance porch
on the road.

Plans of the roofing and the first floor.
Key: 1 entrance 2 portico 3 water garden
4 patio surfaced with gravel 5 grassy embankment
6 deposit.
South front of the water garden and view
of the hypostyle roof.

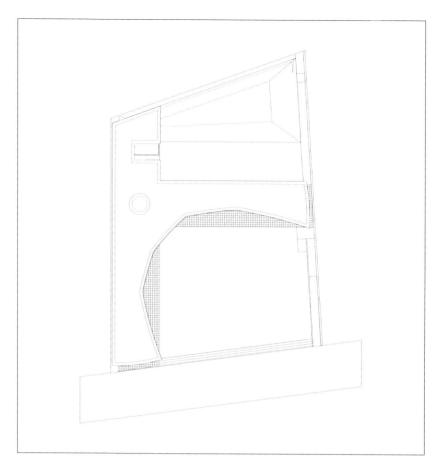

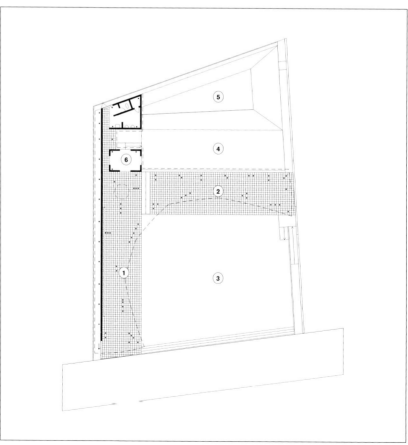

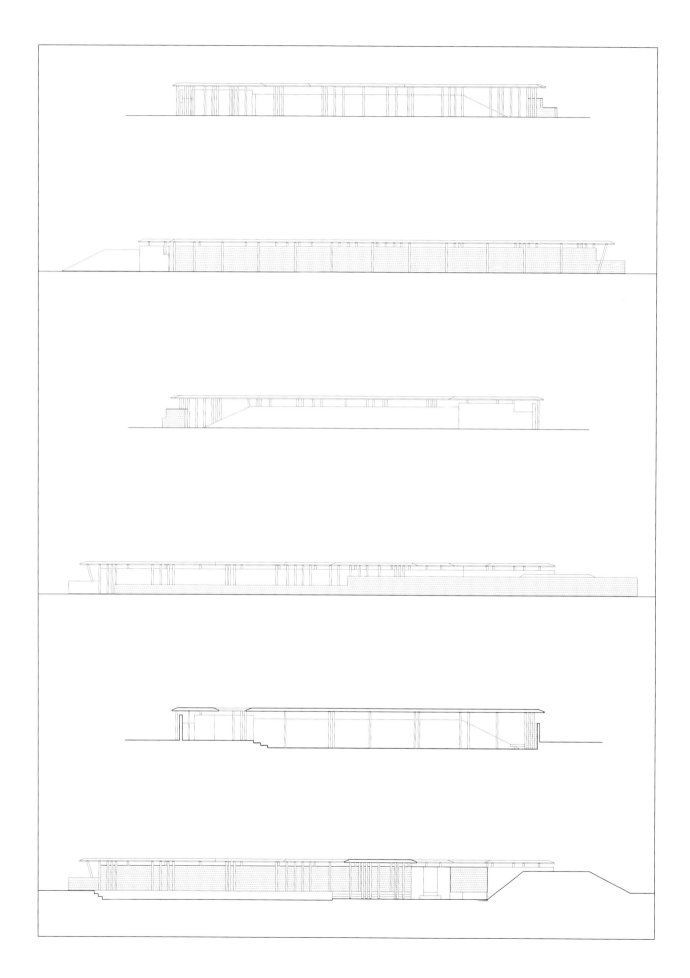

South, west, north and east elevations
and sections.
Detail of the oculus at the corner and the irregular
grouping of the pillars.
Views of the two orthogonal sides of the portico.

Springtecture H
public toilets
Shingu-cho, Hyogo, 1997–98

This is a toilet facility in a small park sited in a densely built-up area in the mountains of Hyogo Prefecture, Japan. It can be reached in one hour by high-speed train from Osaka. As a public amenity of a kind found everywhere in Japan, it avoids any regional character. Located in a park sandwiched between new primary- and secondary-school buildings, the facility has a simple layout. It is divided into three sections: a janitor's room and toilets for men and women.

Public toilets are essential amenities; they need to be accessible, sheltered and safe. This small facility, apparently a simple assemblage of parts, is described as "Halftecture" (half+architecture), because it is both open and closed.

Its openness lies in the fact that it can be traversed in three directions but has no clearly defined entrance. This avoids the defensiveness paradoxically created by demarcated openings and the transparency of glass. In other words the whole facility is a point of passage, with access from almost all sides. On the other hand, it is enclosed spatially by the corrugated steel roofs, walls and floors, to which permeability is added by the double curve of the 3.2 mm thick steel. The basic form of the structure is a rigid spiral of steel sheets supported by steel frames. The architectural concept behind this facility was to create a link between openness and closure through the continuity of the material used. Internal walls turn into ceilings and floors, which continue into external walls and roofs then coil back into the interior.

Interior and exterior merge endlessly into one another, subverting the viewer's expectations and suggesting a new, heterogeneous architectural form created out of the continuous interaction between interior and exterior and role-swapping, in a building made out of materials traditionally used to erect box-shaped buildings.

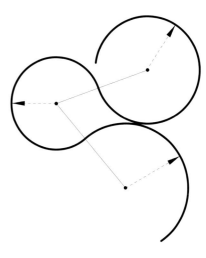

The north-east elevation and one of the three
paths through the building.

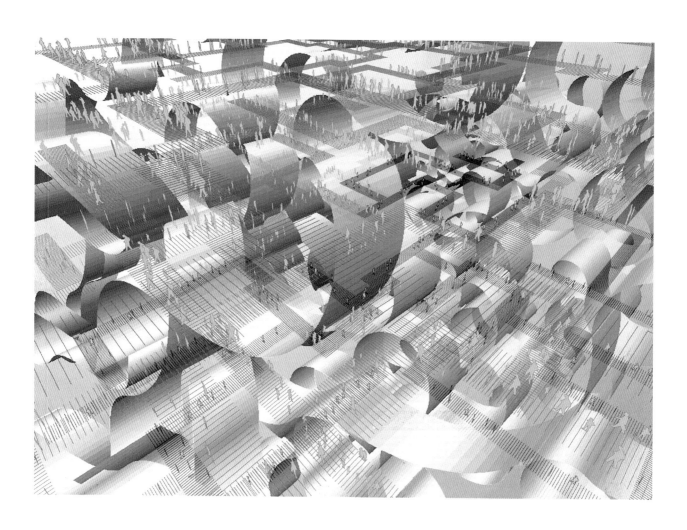

Computer concept of "Springtecture."
East elevation and the interiors of the pavilion.

Plan and diagram of the linear development
of the strip of corrugated steel.
Views of north and south elevations.

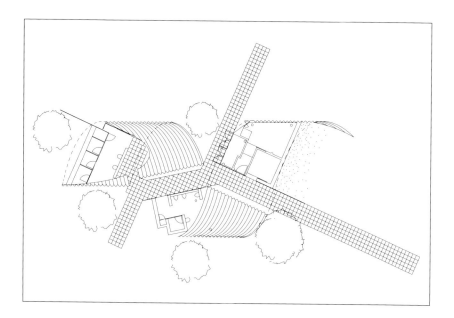

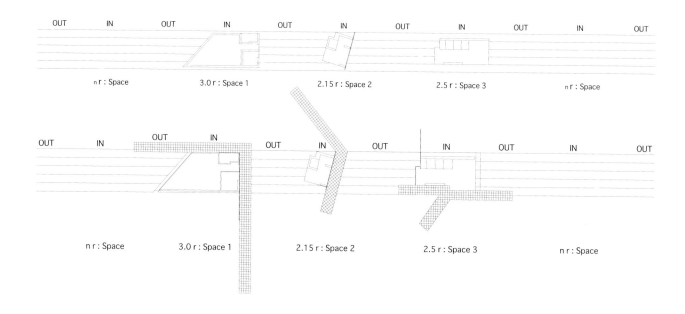

OUT	IN	OUT	IN	OUT	IN	OUT	IN	OUT	IN	OUT

n r : Space   3.0 r : Space 1   2.15 r : Space 2   2.5 r : Space 3   n r : Space

OUT	IN	OUT	IN	OUT	IN	OUT	IN	OUT	IN	OUT

n r : Space   3.0 r : Space 1   2.15 r : Space 2   2.5 r : Space 3   n r : Space

East, north, west, and south elevations.
Details of the structure.

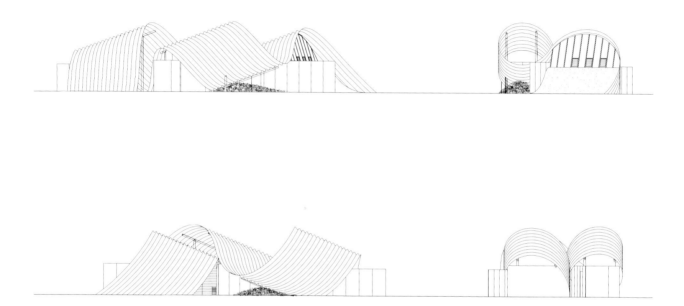

X1   X2   X3   X4   X5   X6   X7   X8   X9   X1 ⟶ X9

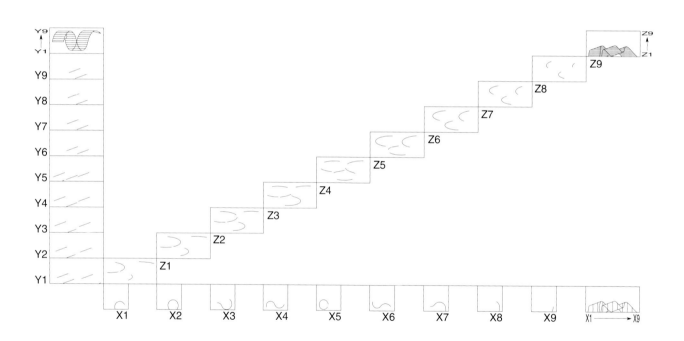

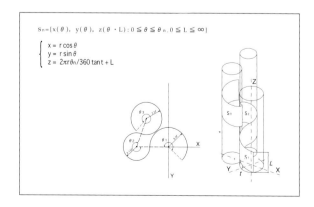

$$S_n = \{x(\theta),\ y(\theta),\ z(\theta \cdot L) : 0 \leqq \theta \leqq \theta_n, 0 \leqq L \leqq \infty\}$$

$$\begin{cases} x = r\cos\theta \\ y = r\sin\theta \\ z = 2\pi r\theta_n/360 \tan t + L \end{cases}$$

Spatial diagram and trigonometric formula
of the curvature.
View of the west front.

Rooftecture N
office block and deposit for building materials
Nishinomiya, Hyogo, 1997–98

This building, located in Nishinomiya, consists of three floors to be used as office space and a temporary deposit for building materials. It stands on the corner of a busy intersection. To prevent it from looming over the street, part of the façade is set back and screened by folding the flat corrugated steel roof back at the front. This enhances the sense of openness at the front of the building and at the same time secures more space housed within fewer building components. The design is an attempt to create a style that can only be achieved through architecture itself: it frees the structure from the limitations of being an assemblage of different components.

The building has a roughly rectangular plan, with a tiny courtyard laid out around a tree at one side. The office and a small conference room on the first level are housed in the south-east wing.

The west side is used as a storehouse and protected from outside by a high roof with generous overhang to facilitate the handling of materials. Three floors providing storage space are linked by staircases set at different points of the building. A wooden hoist-shaft rises through the metal-grid floors. The exteriors are wholly faced with thin silver or black metal panels: the only exception is the main elevation, which is lined with cedar boards.

The building's main function is to provide facilities for handling materials and storing them conveniently. To this end the sturdy, transparent metal grid used for the floors is not only strong enough to support the loads but also enhances the circulation of air, light and sound inside and makes the goods highly visi-

ble. Light from skylights in the roof filters down the whole depth of the building and intersects with horizontal shafts of light cast by long vertical slits in the shell of the building.

The pattern of light is further complicated by the variable arrangement of the piles of material, which provide an immediate image of the logic and dynamics of the business. The high degree of permeability of the metal grids creates the effect of a stratified but coherent interior, clearly showing the power of architecture to define the boundaries of space.

Much of the effectiveness of the result is secured by the curving band of sheet metal that defines half the roof and one outside wall without being either a roof or a wall proper: this continuous surface could be the starting point for a new kind of architecture.

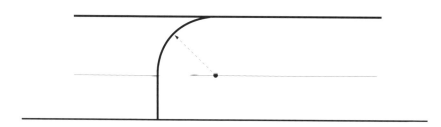

View of the office wing on the east front
of the building.

Plans of the third, second and first floors
and detail of the west front. Key: 1 deposit
2 office 3 conference room.

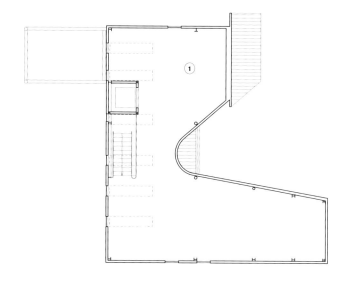

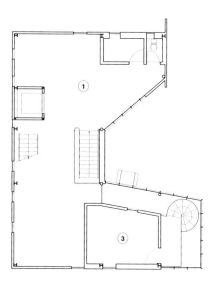

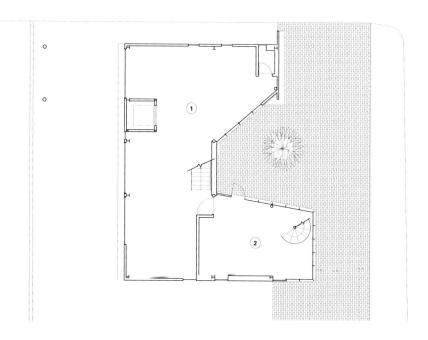

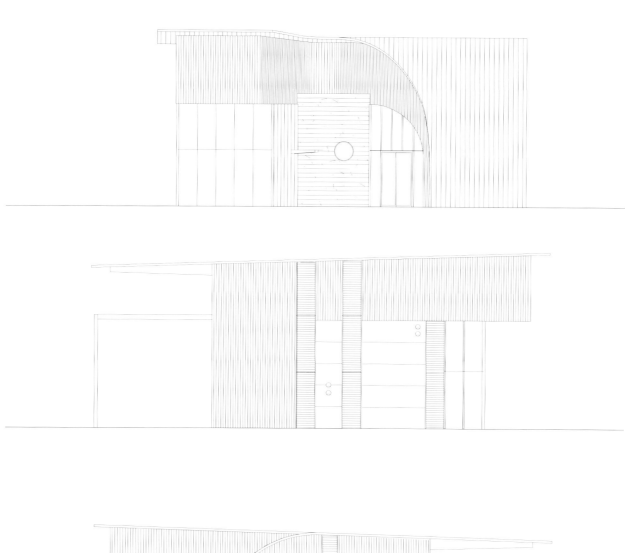

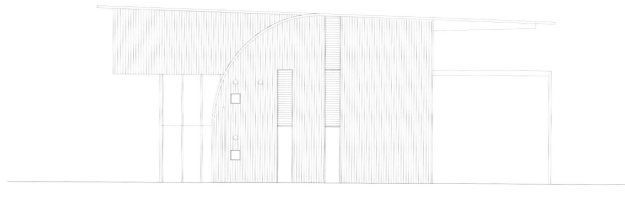

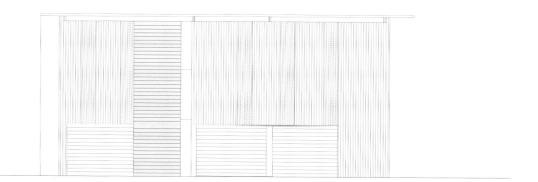

East, south, north and west elevations.
View of the south and west fronts, with roof
overhang to protect loading and unloading.

Longitudinal and cross sections.
Interior views of the storehouse and of the service
staircase leading to the conference room on the
second floor.

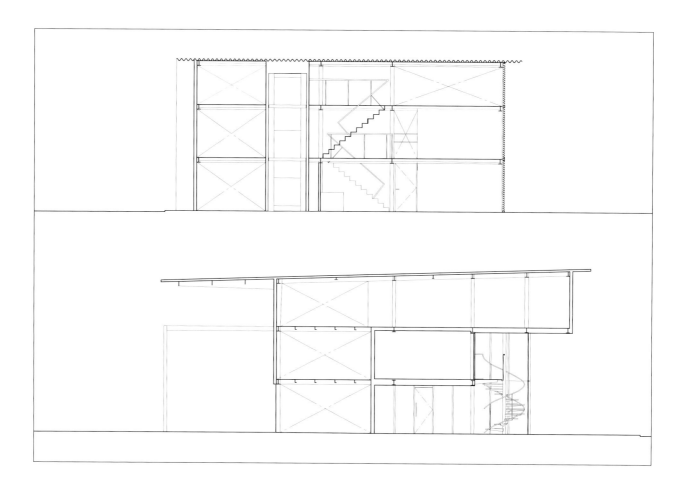

Rooftecture O
cultural center
Shimizu-cho, Fukui, 1996–98

This building stands in a town about three hours by car from Osaka. It was built to house a traditional rite of great antiquity: an important Shintoist ceremony, formerly presented in temples in many parts of Japan.

The inhabitants of Oomori, where the building stands, have perpetuated it, with commendable devotion, for some 800 years. Following a natural catastrophe and a local recession it was decided to create a special public space dedicated to the ritual. The Japanese government has designated the center a national heritage site. It is hoped that the shrine will help revitalize the area, which has an aging population and an economy based on agriculture and forestry.

The community ritual starts at dawn on the morning of February 14 each year, with the removal of a portable shrine from the main hall of the shrine. The residents carry the shrine in procession around the whole community; they then approach a stage inside the building from the south, taking a roundabout route along an old road that starts north of the site. The procession finally enters the building, where the scale of the interiors and the form of the roof reflect the dimensions of the instruments used in the ceremony. Since the entry is made on a diagonal from the south-west, the single great vault of the roof slopes down gradually towards the north-east and to one side. The building has a large hall and various rehearsal rooms for the ceremony. Since it is also used for social functions during the rest of the year, it has a large tatami room and a kitchen.

The ceremony consists of an agricultural fertility rite to ensure abundant harvests. Covering the sacred site with a large roof might have compromised the ceremonial relationship with the sun. However it was decided to cover the whole sacred site since the rite takes place in winter, when the outlines of the building are shrouded with snow.

East front of the building.

General plan, exploded axonometric projection and plan. Key: 1 ceremonial chamber 2 entrance hall 3 route of the ceremony 4 tatami room 5 multi-purpose room 6 public entrance 7 ceremonial entrance 8 information 9 kitchen 10 outdoor exhibition space.
Detail of the entrance porch and view of the south front.

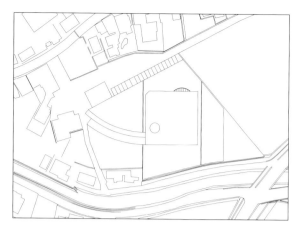

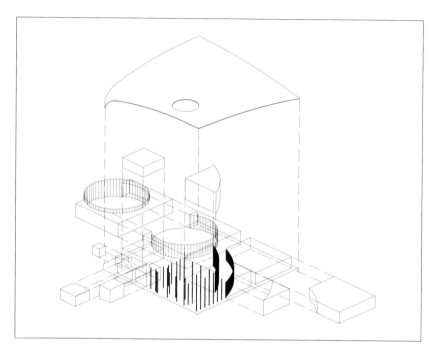

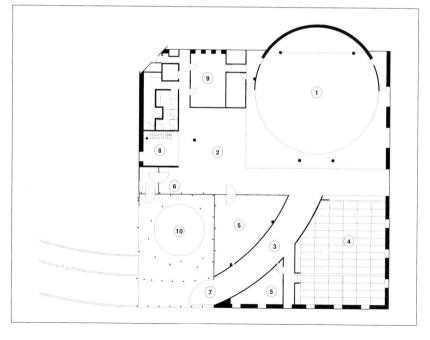

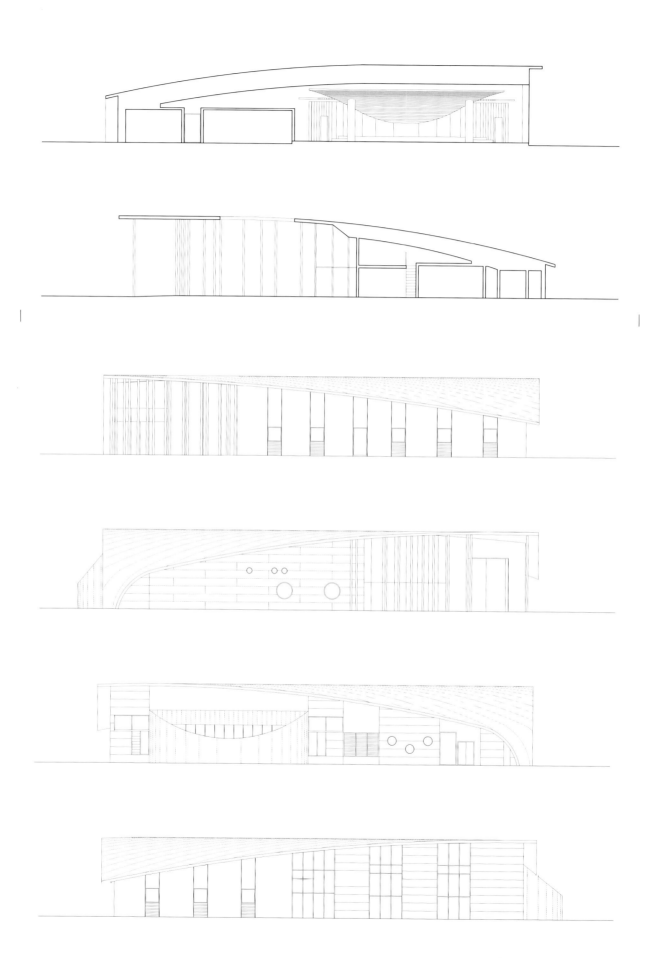

Longitudinal sections through the ceremonial hall,
and cross section through the vestibule.
South, west, north and east elevations.
Interior views of the ceremonial hall and
of the stage.

Rooftecture H
office building
Himeji, Hyogo, 1996–98

This project is for an office building in a small town around an hour from Osaka by train. It is the headquarters of a co-operative of over 100 companies and receives numerous visitors. For this reason an open single-story design was adopted, with a high degree of over-hang to shelter access to the car park, which is on street level. The interior also has an open layout, with airy, luminous public areas, a lobby and an atrium that ties the spaces together. The first three floors are made of reinforced concrete; the fourth floor and roof rest on a steel frame.

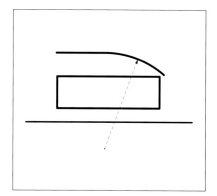

South-east corner of the building and the east façade.

North, south, west and east elevations.
Main entrance and view of the east front.

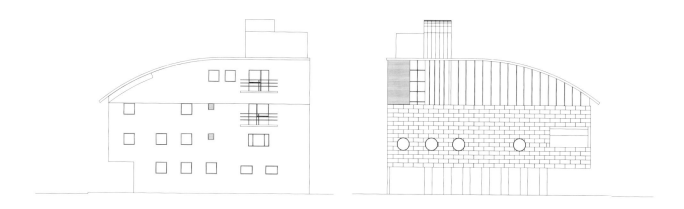

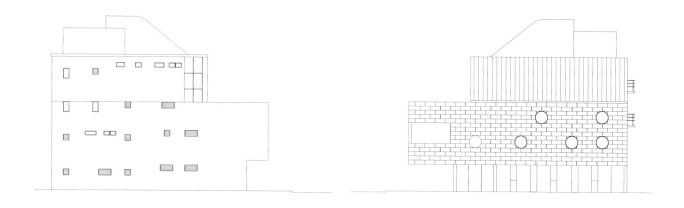

Sections and views of interiors of the central
atrium and of the assembly room on the third floor.

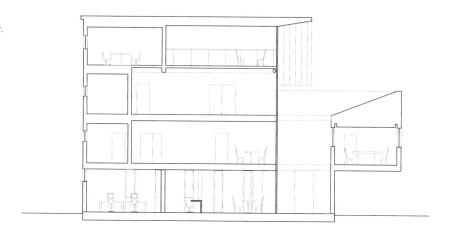

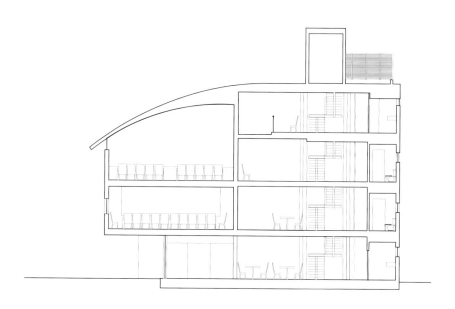

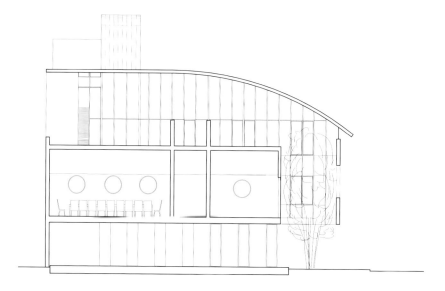

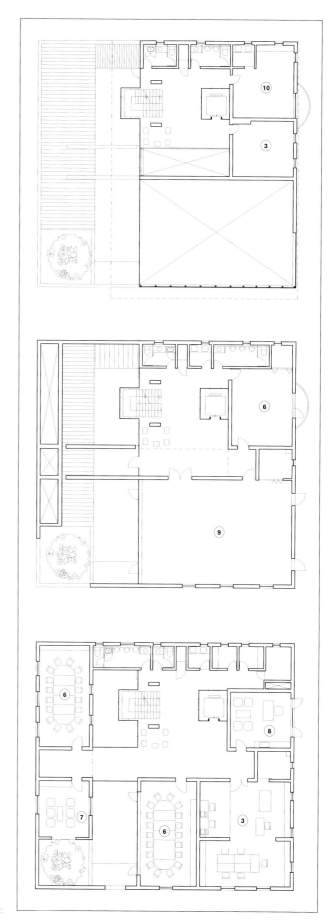

Plans of first, fourth, third and second floors.
Key: 1 entrance 2 hall 3 office 4 CAD room
5 courtyard 6 conference room 7 waiting room
8 president's office 9 conference room
10 common room.
Details of the roofing and the glass-covered
stairwell in the atrium.

Rooftecture Y
health spa
Yamasaki-cho, Hyogo, 1997–98

This health spa stands in a small mountain village called Yoi, about an hour's drive from Osaka.

The facility consists of two blocks combined and integrated to form a single linear building. One block houses baths for men, women and the physically disabled, the other an office and other collective spaces.

"Rooftecture" is a term coined for this kind of structure: not a roofing system but a way of securing the requisite functional qualities by uniting two buildings. Each of the rooms corresponds to a specific roof area that defines its volume, while it is also integrated into the building's continuous outer shell. Supported by a steel frame, the outer shell is not in this case a self-supporting structure: its function is to unite and articulate the rooms. Rooftecture combines the essential parts of the two blocks to form a coordinated combination of external and internal spaces. In the early planning stage it was decided to provide numerous windows on the south side, facing a valley, to let in plenty of sunlight and enable visitors to enjoy the splendid natural landscape.

To enhance the view, despite the extent of the site, the complex was built on a small ridge at the top of the property. Because of the length of the façade, with its long row of windows running from east to west, the western end of the building juts out beyond the ridge. The overhang is supported by the machine room, which forms an artificial foundation for the men's bath above. A cavity in the ceiling secures ventilation. The collective spaces, including the office and lobby, are set in the north wing of the complex facing the road. Designed with consideration for the site's natural landforms, the two blocks are linked by a corridor that runs from the entrance and lounge through their point of intersection.

The open layout of these partially interlocking volumes, without any intermediate supports, made it easier to design their essential internal spaces and provide numerous additional rooms between them. The linear form of the outer shell linking the two buildings is reflected in the continuous line of flow through the interior.

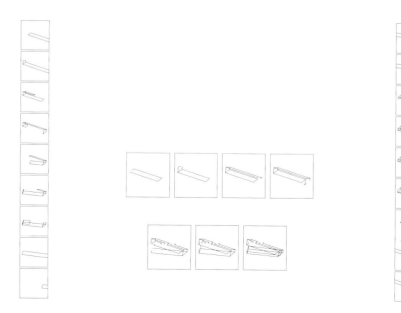

North front facing the road.

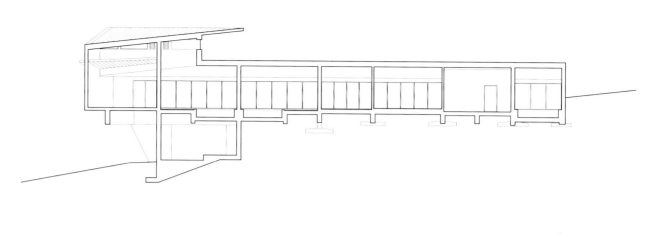

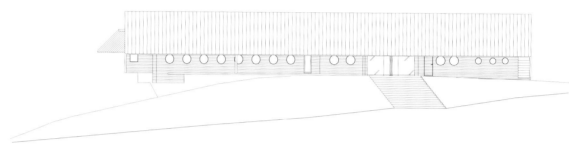

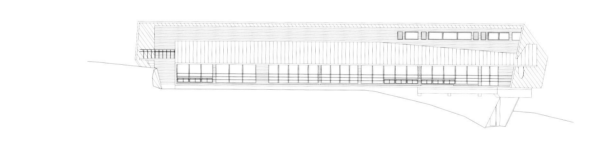

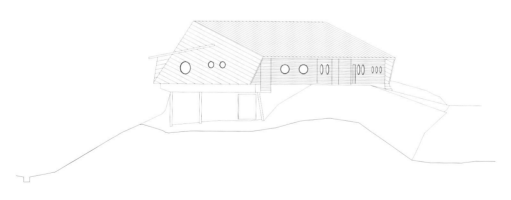

Longitudinal section of the south wing and north,
south, east and west elevations.
Central courtyard of the south front.

Following pages
The building in its mountain setting.

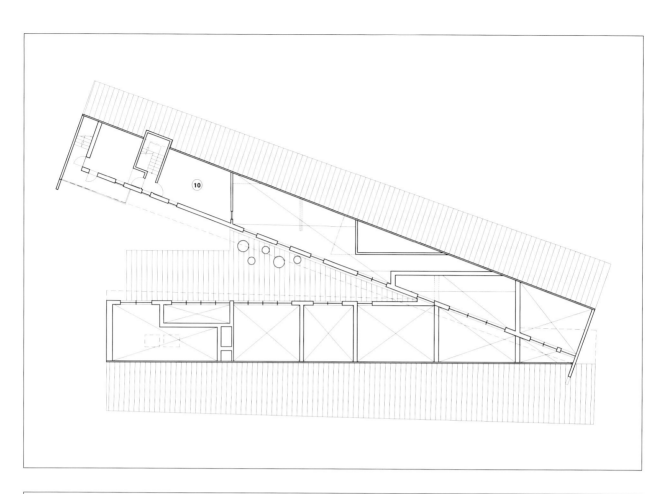

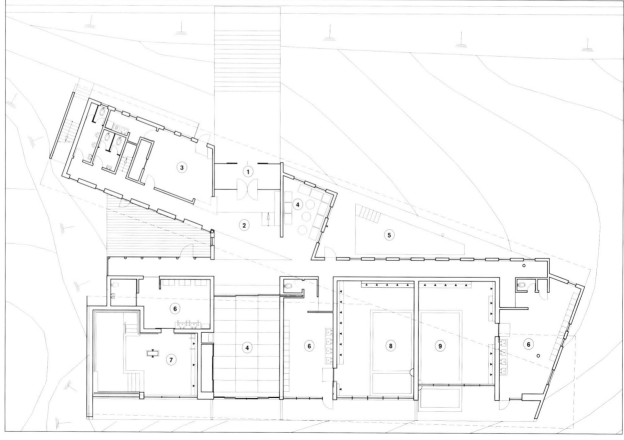

Plans of the second and first floors.
Key: 1 entrance 2 hall 3 office 4 waiting room
5 pool 6 locker room 7 bath for the disabled
8 women's bath 9 men's bath 10 storeroom.
The entrance hall and the women's bath.

Springtecture A
competition project for an art museum
Aomori, 1999–2000

This project was an entry in the first phase of a competition for an art museum in north-eastern Japan. The basic idea was to create a type of architecture based on geometrical regularity, despite its irregular appearance. This approach was originally explored in "Springtecture H." The brief called for a complex sequence of spaces and facilities: the design provides them by using linear structures made from strips of sheet metal jointed to form continuous curved surfaces. A number of these structures are set parallel to each other and connected at short intervals, with metal spirals coiling from inside to out and from outside to in to enfold both interiors and exteriors in a versatile unity. Five continuous rolls of curved sheet steel are integrated in a compositional scheme that furnishes all the areas required in the plan and the required heights in section. Structurally, the buildings are made of curved pre-cast panels of reinforced concrete connected in sequence. The project aimed to create a lively multi-functional architecture disciplined by a rigorous geometrical order without being either monotonous or banal.

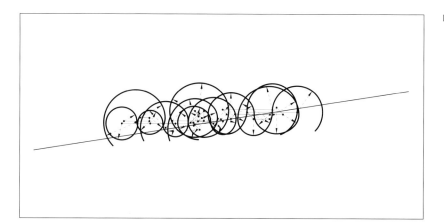

Detail of the computer model.

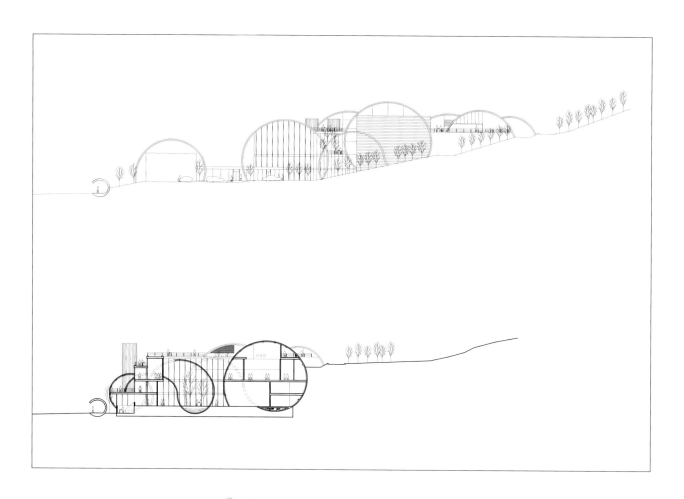

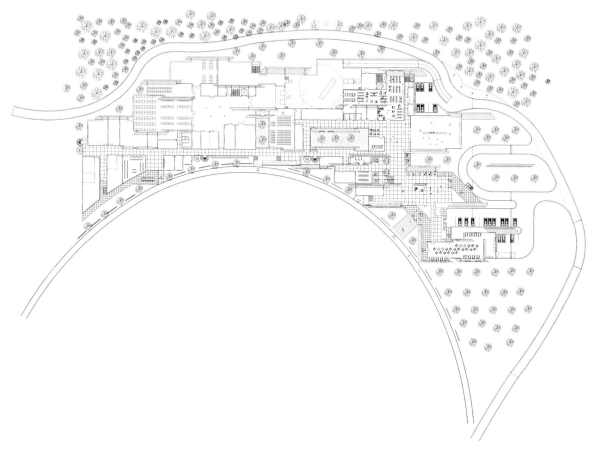

West elevation, cross section and plan of the first floor.
Views of exterior and interior in the computer model.

99

Springtecture NHK

competition project for an ecological house
Inagi, Tokyo, 1999

This model ecological house was designed to be made of sheets of corrugated steel. They are a standard factory product that can be moved without using machinery and simply bolted together. Using them as the primary building material minimizes waste and energy consumption on the building site. Then the steel sheets can be recycled in a blast furnace or dismantled for use in another building with a different form. A continuous surface ("Renzokutai") of double steel sheets makes for a strong structure and leaves large openings for windows to capture plenty of light and air. The cavity between the double metal sheets can be used to circulate water, cooled in the basement or warmed by the sun, to regulate the temperature indoors.

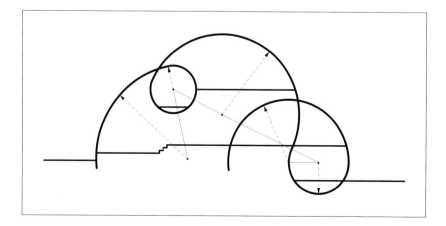

Views of the computer model.

Longitudinal section and plans of the second
and first floors.
Views of the interior modelled on the computer.

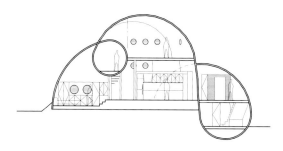

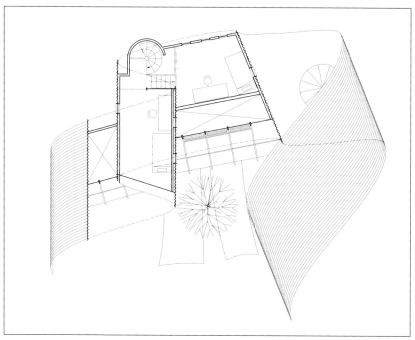

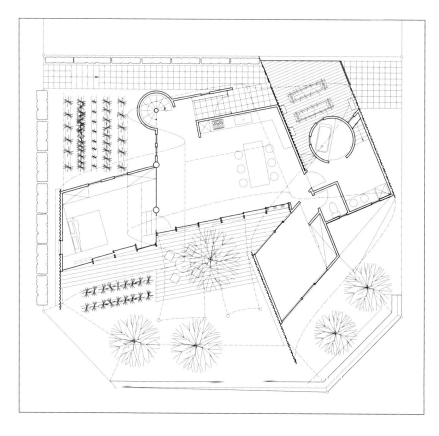

Springtecture I
2000

"Springtecture" is an architectural system for the immediate future. A strip of sheet steel bounds the space between the volutes of a coiled and spiraling surface. The continuous strip of material with a constant section woven into spirals is combined with different degrees of openness and closure to generate discontinuous forms. No cultural factors, creative impulses, personal feelings or thoughts affect the intelligibility of the structure. "Springtecture" is a building system that enables us to recognize each other unconsciously in the thin corrugated surface.

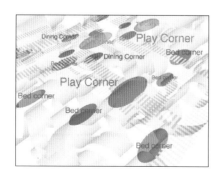
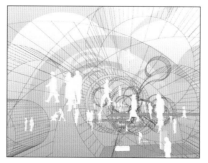

Computer concept of the architectural and spatial system.

Rooftecture K
office building
Nishinomiya, Hyogo, 1998–2000

This building, the headquarters of a construction company, faces a busy street in Nishinomiya city. On the south and west of the site are some rather featureless buildings that offer little in the way of rapport. On the north side is the main road. But beyond the road appears a beautiful range of mountains with Mount Rokko. Four continuous curved steel sheets define a three-story volume. Part of the first floor has been left open to form a service court with parking space for four cars. The hallway is completely transparent and the straight metal staircase, with treads made of a steel grid, is visible from outside. On the second floor there is an office for ten staffmembers. The third floor, set under the broad roof, has a conference room and the president's office. The roof begins as a continuous wall that forms one side of the building and then folds over and covers it above.

View of the north front.

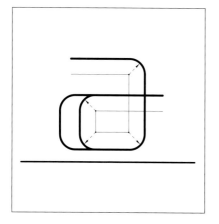

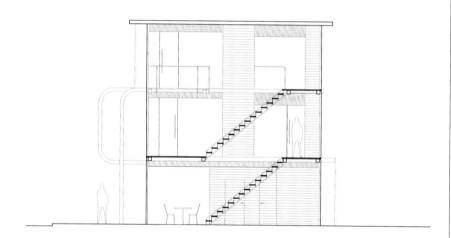

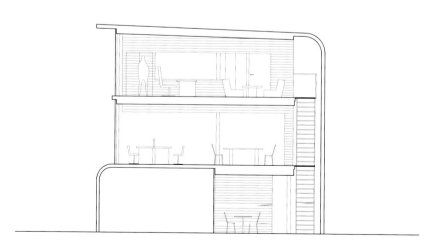

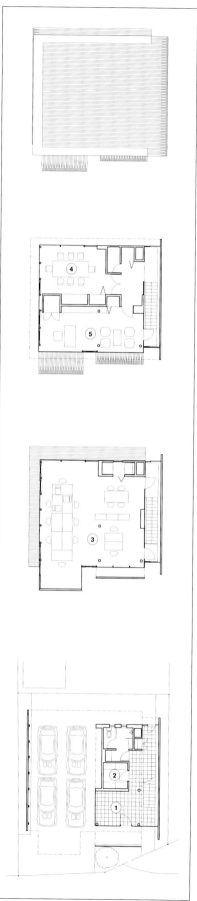

Cross section through the stair block
and longitudinal section. Plans of the roofing
and the third, second and first floors.
Key: 1 hall 2 wardrobe 3 office 4 conference
rooms 5 president's office.
General view and detail of the front facing
the road.

Detail of the projecting volumes on the north front, office space on the second floor and view of the staircase in the steel grid at the side.

Rooftecture B
farm emporium
Biwa-cho, Shiga, 1998–2000

This small emporium stands on the road skirting Lake Biwa in the north of Shiga Prefecture. It is immersed in the peace of an extensive lakeside and rural area. The building is divided into three parts and includes a shop (lot A), a store for stocking and selling farm produce (lot B), and a small processing plant for producing fruit juice, ice-cream, etc. The different functions complement each other.

Construction was divided into two phases and it was decided to complete lot C only after completing lots A and B. In this broad, open landscape, it was important to confer unity on the fragmentary complex by means of a continuous roof. The triangular site is made up of three rectangular lots forming a single area. A distinctive feature is that each side faces a different view. The south fronts the busy lakeside road, across which is a beach used by bathers. An access road is ruled out here; at most the emporium gets some customers who stroll over from the lakefront. On the north side there is a small residential complex; on this side the emporium has a bay for delivering farm produce and an entrance for the local inhabitants. The road on the east side has been laid out with facilities for motorists from outside the district. To cope with these factors, the store was set off axis, aligned with the southern boundary of the site, with the sale of farm produce in the north-west corner and the processing plant in the north-east. This layout left some spaces free and access to each section open and differentiated.

The three blocks were completed and united by a corrugated metal wall-roof supported by a steel and timber frame. Complex patterns are created by the simple arrangement of the continuous metal roofing, which is partly shared by the various facilities.

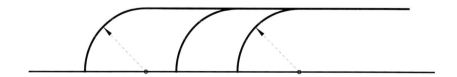

Image and reverse angle of the north front
of the building.

Computer model of the project concept.
Details of north and south front.

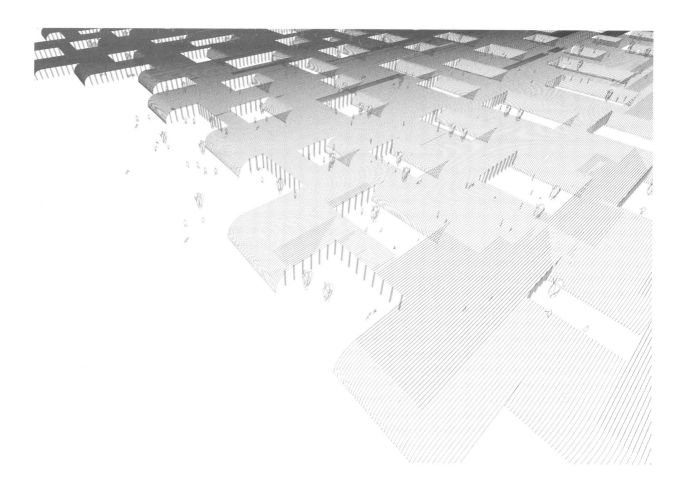

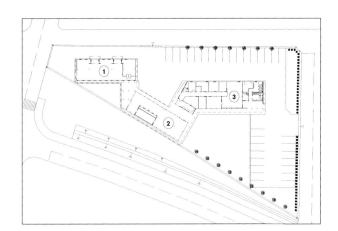

Plan of the first floor; plan of the lot.
Key: 1 store for farm produce 2 shop
3 produce processing plant.
Longitudinal and cross sections of the shop,
farm produce store, and processing plant.
View of interior of the processing plant.

Rooftecture A
apartment block
Taitou-ku, Tokyo, 1998–2000

Two families, a young couple and their parents, live in this building. The four-story block is divided between them. In a crowded neighborhood, the parents live in the two floors at the top, which are quiet, comfortable and served by an inside elevator.

On the "flagpole" lot, the "flag" part is occupied by the house and the "pole" part is designated as a parking space for two cars. The second floor of the building juts out, in compliance with a local planning regulation, to create a sheltered entrance close to the street. The interior is shared by the two families. The property is closely surrounded by high-density apartment blocks. Normally the building next door would be set close to the windows, so the architect set the apartment block slightly closer to the north side of the lot to increase the clearance in front of the windows. The roof and walls of the stairwell are transparent, so creating a shaft of natural light that illuminates all the interiors.

View of the north front of the house.

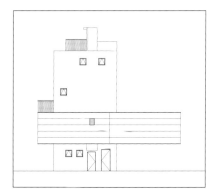

Plans of the first, fourth, third and second floors.
Details of the tatami room in the projecting volume.

Following pages
Third floor living room.

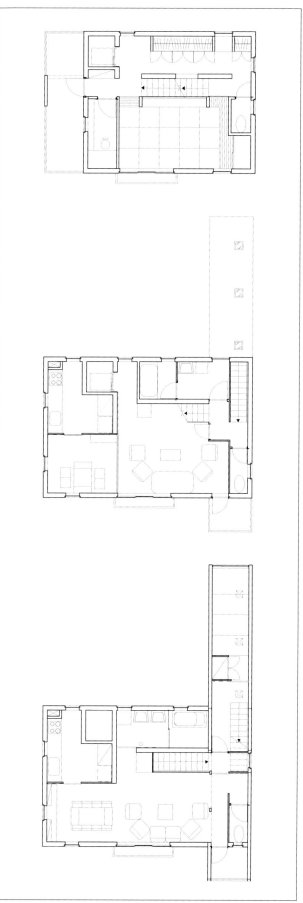

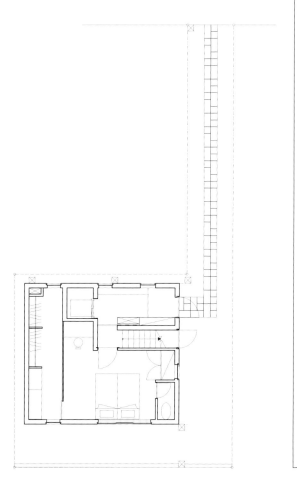

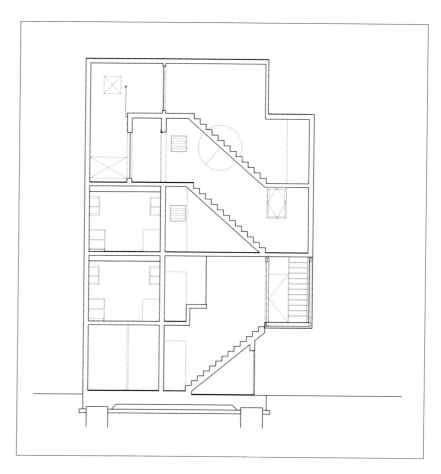

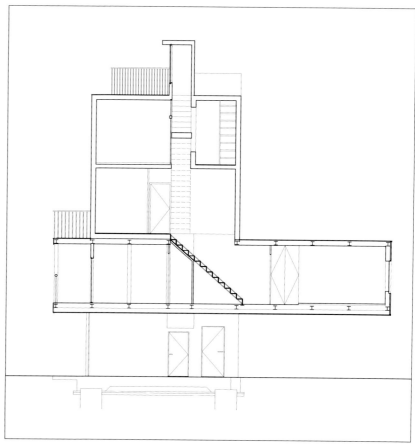

Longitudinal sections, cross section.
Flight of stairs to the attic.

Rooftecture WIPO

competition project
Geneva, Switzerland, 1999–2000

This project was entered in the first phase of a competition for an extension to the headquarters of the World Intellectual Property Organization (WIPO) in Geneva. The complex brief called for a large number of underground parking lots, a large conference hall and office space. The basic concept behind this project was that the architecture should epitomize WIPO's activities. It was thought that the structure of DNA would provide an apt structural system. The potential of humanity is based on the versatility of multicultural societies and the ways they interact. There is a close analogy between this and the regularity and diversity of characters in DNA, a principle common to all living things. Guided by this insight, the project is based on a grid of load-bearing walls and pre-cast floor-slabs, the latter containing cavities to house the ducts for wiring and air-conditioning. This all-purpose construction system, which generates a wide range of configurations and flexible spaces, was combined with continuous sheet-metal roofing that confers unity on the building.

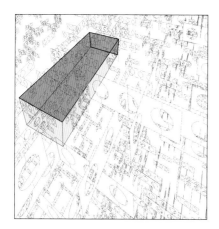
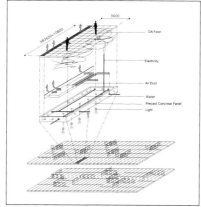

Project concept and scheme of the modular
building system.
Photo-montage of the building's insertion on
the project and detail of the catwalk connecting
with the WIPO tower.

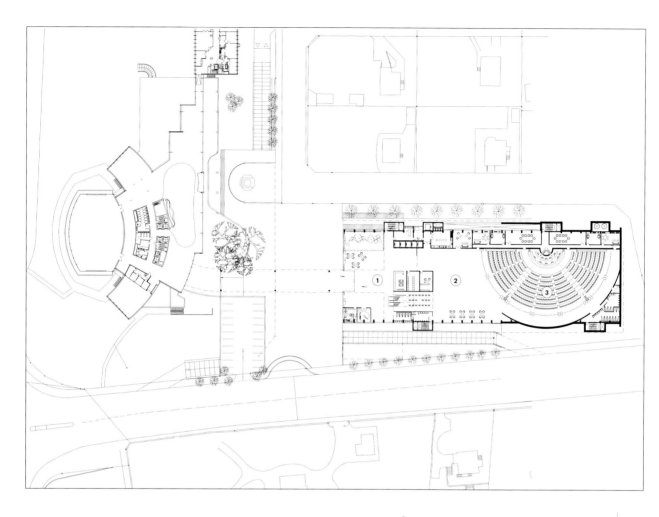

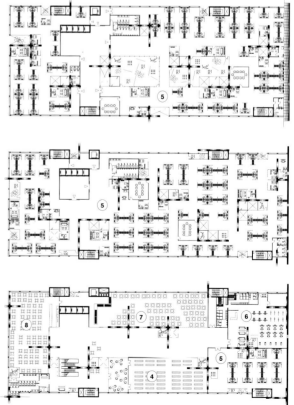

General plan at grade and plans of the fifth,
third and second floors. Key: 1 hall 2 foyer
3 conference rooms 4 library 5 offices 6 gym
7 cafeteria 8 self-service restaurant.
Longitudinal and cross sections of the north-east
elevation.

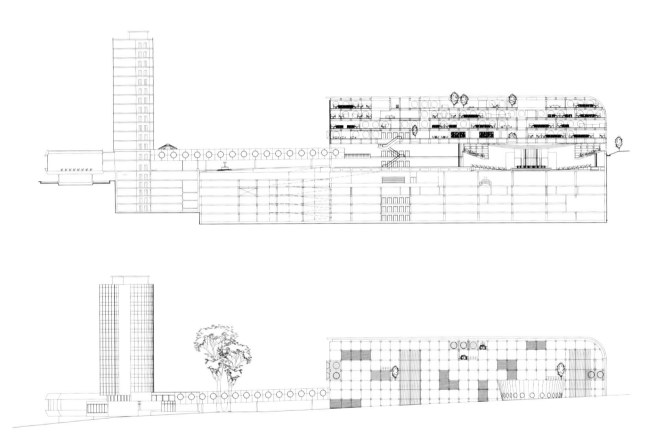

Springtecture Orléans
temporary installation
Orléans, France, 1999–2000

This structure was designed as a display at Archilab, an exhibition held in Orléans, France. It was a temporary installation, exhibited only for the duration of the event. It is composed as a "Halftecture," i.e. it is not divided into clearly differentiated internal and external spaces. The use of corrugated steel gives it structural integrity, and the momentum of its "Renzokutai" (continuity) is developed through a potentially endless series of curves. It offers a practical way to shape three-dimensional architectural spaces that break up the uniformity of a homogeneous urban fabric dominated by Euclidian geometry.

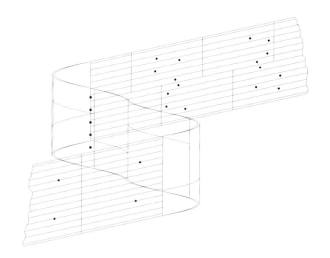

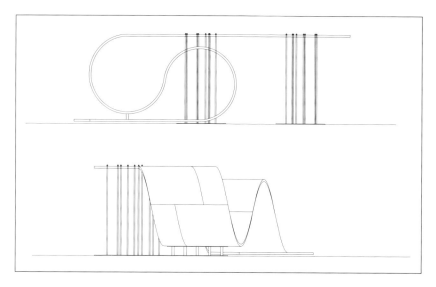

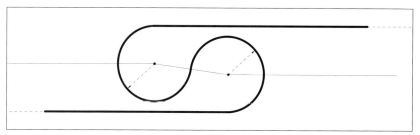

Plan and elevations.
The installation in its setting.

Springtecture S
competition project for a ferry terminal
Sasebo, Nagasaki, 2000–01

This is a competition project for a new ferry terminal for a small town in Nagasaki Prefecture. It shows how to obtain the requisite number of spaces using a single continuous strip-shaped wrapper. To cut construction times, precast concrete panels were chosen for the structure. Two standard types of curved slabs secure continuity between the parts of the building in the cyclical reversal of spiraling surfaces; at the same time they connect interiors and exteriors, replicating and varying the spaces.

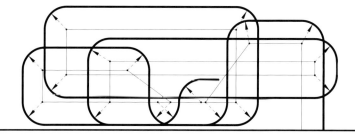

The computer model.

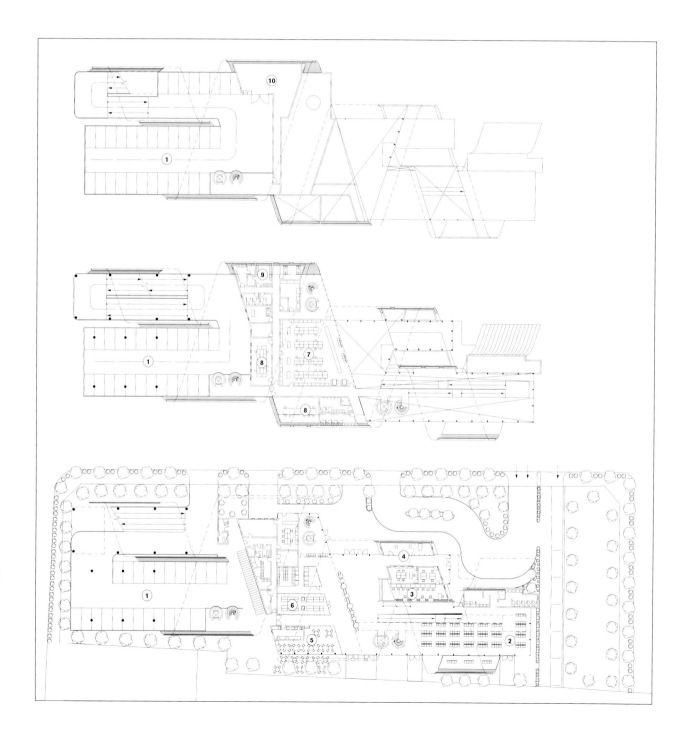

Longitudinal section and plans of the third, second
and first floors. Key: 1 car parks 2 waiting room
3 ticket office 4 information bureau 5 restaurant
6 shop 7 office 8 conference room 9 locker
rooms 10 technical plant.
Computer concept of the project.

Rooftecture Wave
canopy for a used-car lot
Minou, Osaka, 2000–01

The site, about a thirty-minute drive from central Osaka, fronts a major road with heavy traffic. The facility is a used-car display and offices, on a lot surrounded by high-rise buildings lining the straight main road. The display area is sheltered by a long canopy roof, a "Renzokutai" (a continuous ribbon structure). Its profile is made from a modulated sequence of segments of a circle supported on branched pillars to form square grids, each proportioned to the length of an automobile. The design exploits the rigidity of the corrugated metal surface to eliminate cross-beams: the canopy rests directly on the uprights. The sinuous pattern of the canopy contrasts with the monotonously orthogonal urban fabric all around it.

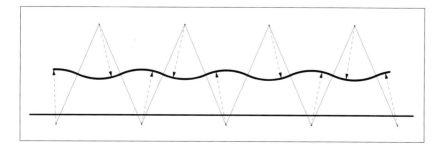

The urban front facing south and detail
of the branching pillars.

Plan and east, west and south elevations.
Key: 1 display 2 offices.
Views of the canopy.

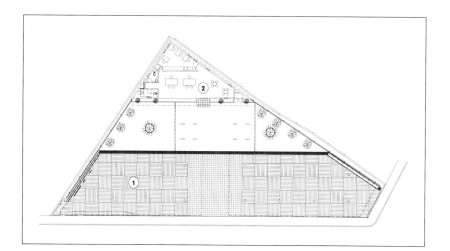

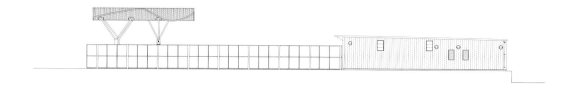

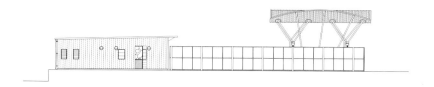

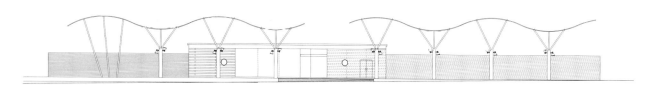

Rooftecture U
factory and offices
Oku-cho, Okayama, 1999–2001

This complex consists of a factory and detached office block for a firm that makes brake shoes for rolling stock. It is located in a typical Japanese farming district with open rice paddies set against a distant mountain range.

A preliminary constraint was the new automated assembly line, which defined the internal volume. The principal difficulty was how to create a unified volume without barriers inside. This was achieved by making the two roofs different heights and giving them different inclinations. The horizontal strip that joins the two roof ridges has a row of louver windows set in the upper part of the south elevation to let in abundant light and air and secure healthy, comfortable working conditions. Facing the factory is a block containing offices, a locker room for the factory workers and cooking facilities for the employees.

The structure is made up of two continuous shed roofs made of corrugated steel set up against each other and partly interlocking. The apertures running along the side of the building are closed with strip windows or wooden boards. The interiors are airy and varied. Illumination of constant brightness is provided by a high skylight facing north that runs the whole length of the factory, from an office on one side to the far end of the main corridor.

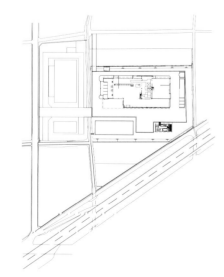

Plan and general view of the complex.

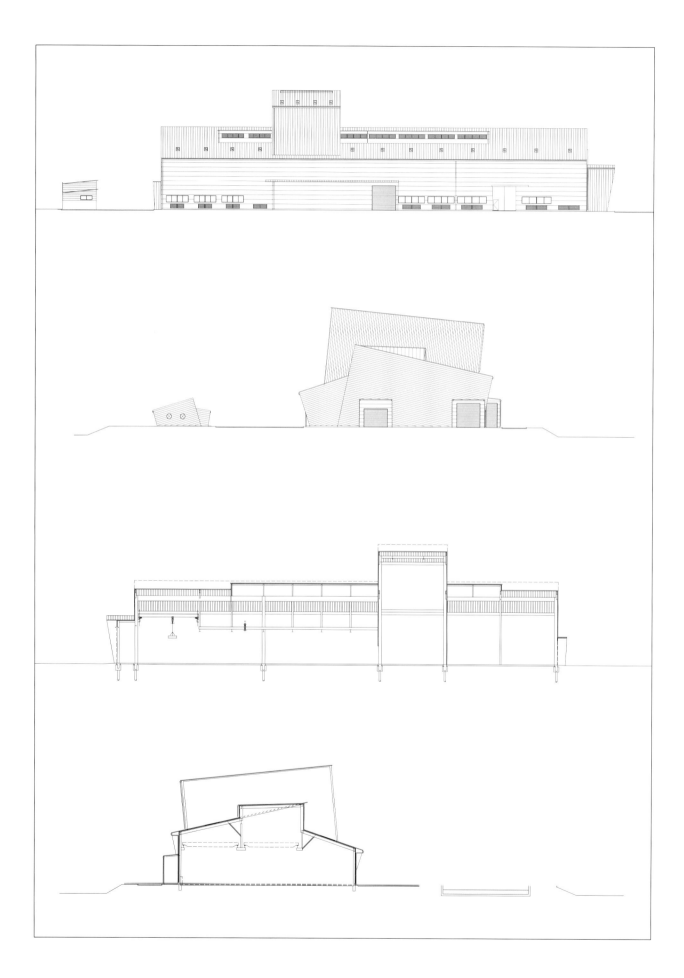

North and east elevations and sections through
the factory.
View of the south front.

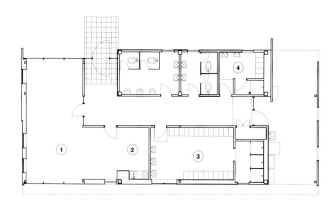

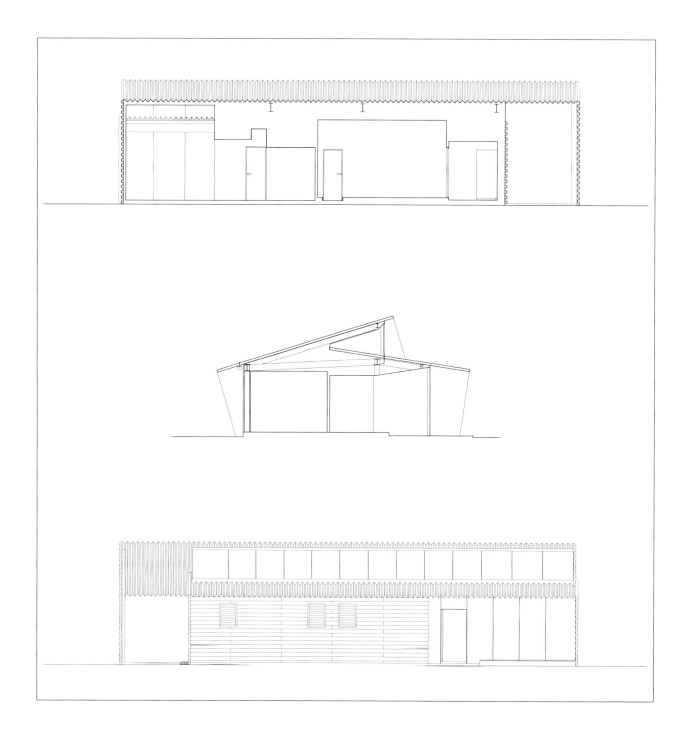

Plan, sections and north elevation of the office
block. Key: 1 office 2 kitchen 3 men's locker
room 4 women's locker room.
North front and view of the central corridor
that distributes the spaces.

Rooftecture M
office-home
Maruoka-cho, Fukui, 2000–01

This is a private house which contains the client's office. It stands in a rather anonymous residential area of a small town three hours by train from Osaka. The lot, set on a north-south axis, forms an elongated rectangle with narrow frontage on a quiet back street; the other sides are hemmed in by neighboring houses.

The client's first request was for an office: it was expected to receive a steady stream of clients. A second request was that the domestic spaces should be secluded and screened from outsiders.

Rooftecture M has the form of a single sheet of material folded over with a cut-out piece in the shape of a saddle: this forms a single continuous wall-roof surface that defines the required volume. There are different points of access to its tunnel-space for the various functions. The office on the second floor front, with a bathroom and a private room, form so many rectangular solids slotted into position along the longitudinal axis. The living, dining and other family rooms mesh with these volumes. The pattern of apertures for windows and doors, to provide the required quantities of light and air inside, can easily be altered by cutting out new openings in the metal envelope.

The design grew out of the basic idea of fashioning the walls and roof as a single element. This meant reducing the architectural space to a strong, continuous surface enveloping a fluid, unified space. In this respect Rooftecture M is a versatile container, wholly inhabitable and serving to support and define the rooms inside. It houses the family as a continuous partly shared structure and shapes a domestic setting that fosters multiple relationships.

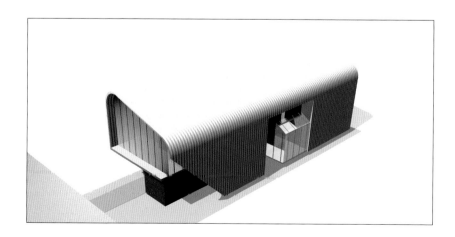

Axonometric projection of the house and detail
of the north end.

Plans of the second and first floors; north
and south elevations.
The north front on the road.

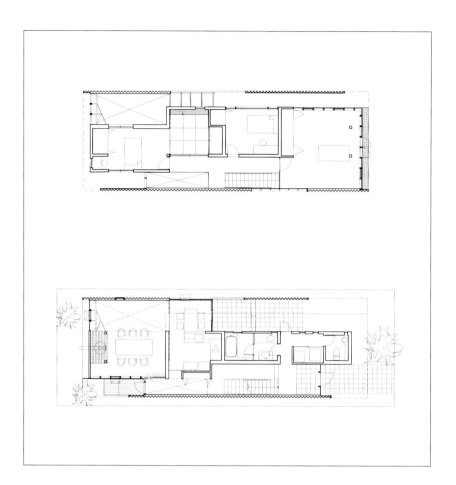

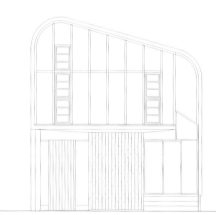

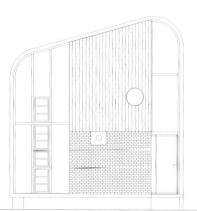

住いの提案

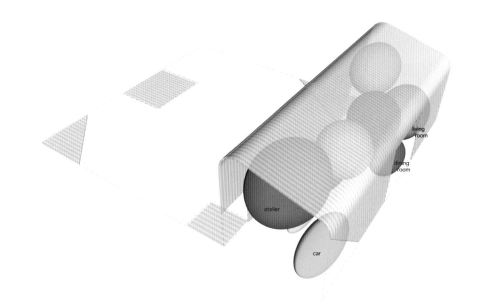

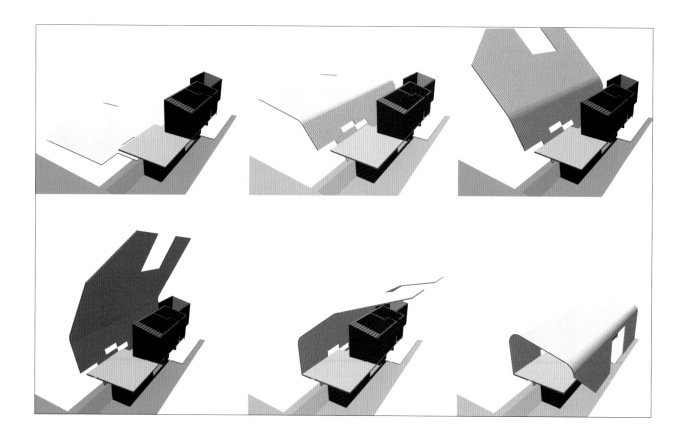

Concept of the project and exploded axonometric projections of the house enveloped in the sheet-steel membrane.
Second-floor office and detail of living room on the first floor.

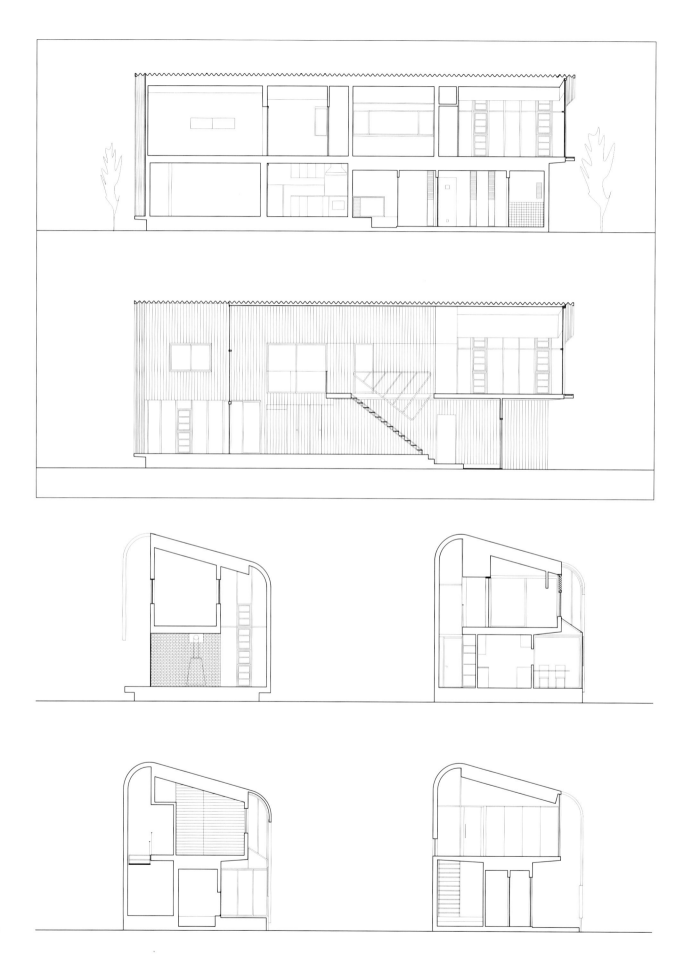

Cross sections.
The dining room seen from the living room; detail
of the stairs to the office.

Rooftecture C
crematorium
Taishi-cho, Hyogo, 2000–

A crematorium marks the boundary between the world in which we live and the world after death. In Japan, mourning signifies "bidding farewell to the dead as they depart for the other world." A crematorium is thus a threshold, a space for last goodbyes. This structure was designed as four curved surfaces.

The first large curved surface is the outer wall and marks the boundary between interior and exterior. The entrance is a slit in this blind wall. Spanning the entrance, a second vaulted surface defines an intermediate area. The third is the large arched roof, which rises to embrace a capacious volume and represents the sorrow of parting. The passage that leads back from the hall to the exterior is defined by the last convex wall. When combined, the four curved surfaces create a space for bidding farewell to the dead as they depart to another world.

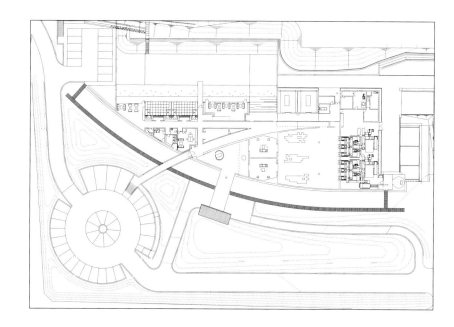

General plan.
View of the interior and the model.

Rooftecture Rome
project for a residential complex
Rome, Italy, 2001

This project for central Rome was an attempt to furnish the right kind of high-density urban housing for the twenty-first century by adding new elements to a number of apartment blocks that still bear the scars of World War II. The brief called for shops and offices on the first floors of the additions and housing on the upper floors. The design starts, horizontally, by opening up a linked series of hallways and, vertically, by inserting a kinetic network of tubular connections between one building and another. The object of the project is to arouse a sense of shared awareness and bring a new feeling of community to high-density housing.

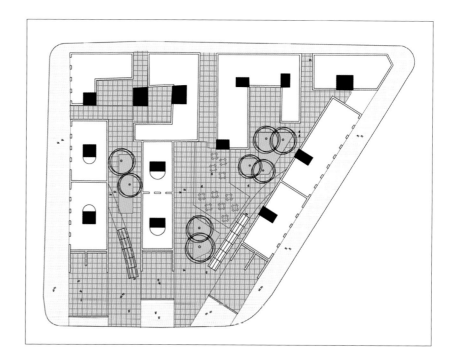

View of the first floor and views
of the computer model.

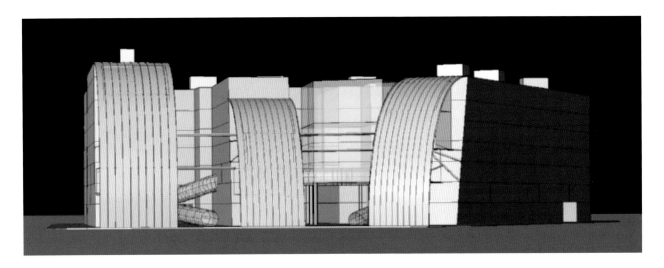

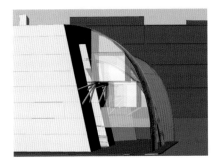

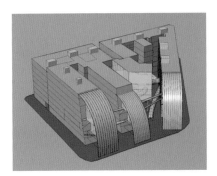

Osaka Apartments
apartment complex
Katano, Osaka, 2000–

This is a plan for rebuilding a high-density housing project for low-income groups. At present the material poverty of the inhabitants of the complex is compensated for by the rich community life they share.

The first step in the redesign was to define the minimum space needed to satisfy each resident's needs, then this unit was multiplied by their total number. Establishing a planar "Renzokutai" ("continuity") for this structure entailed variations in the uniform residential units. "Renzokutai" develops longitudinally through the building, forming the roof, wall and floor, so that it is partly shared by each of the home units. This project was an experiment in "Bunyutai" (partial sharing) to define a complex made up of parts that share the whole. "Bunyutai" is an image of belonging; it transcribes and reinforces the sense of rapport created spontaneously within the community by the residents themselves.

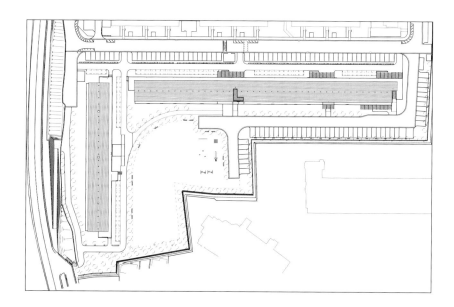

General plan and computer model of the
"Renzokutai" aggregation of the home units.

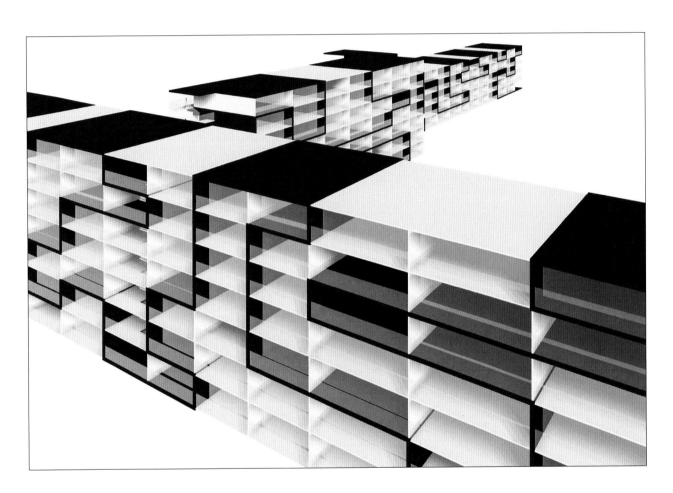

Bubbletecture M

kindergarten
Maihara-cho, Shiga, 2001–

This kindergarten is about 45 minutes by train from Osaka, on the Shinkansen line. It is set in the middle of a recent housing development. The structure consists of a series of alternating concrete blocks and classrooms, with a wooden roof that unites the blocks. The shell-shaped roof is a faceted continuous surface made up of triangular elements. Its structural strength and geometrical consistency allow for great freedom in the configuration of spaces. The three-dimensional grid system, prefabricated and simply assembled on site, is based on wooden posts 2.5 meters long and hexagonal metal struts. The integration of the wooden frame with the concrete blocks is controlled by a stringent geometrical logic but it produces richly expressive architecture.

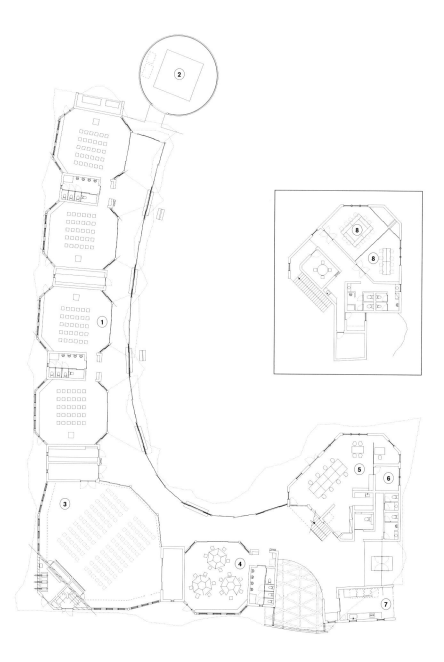

Plans of first and second floors of the offices.
Key: 1 classroom 2 swimming pool 3 games
room 4 reception room 5 staff room 6 infirmary
7 kitchen 8 conference room.
Sections and west, south, east and north
elevations.

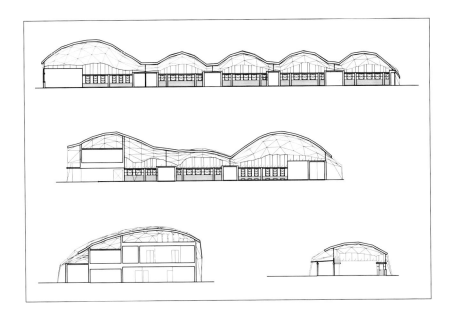

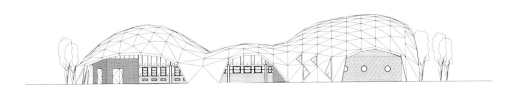

161

Rooftecture S
office building
Osaka, 2001–

This building in downtown Osaka is the headquarters of a major corporation. The client wanted a functional layout on each floor as well as a corporate image that would express the coordinated unity of its multiple operations. The architectural response was a series of traditional structural elements forming a continuous line zigzagging across the whole building. The line rises up the west elevation, with a porch at the side that rises three stories high. The wall then turns to form the floor of the fifth story, where it reaches its maximum horizontal extension. It becomes the dividing wall between the fifth floor and the open stairwell linking the second floor to the third and fourth. It then runs downward before turning at the third floor to form the ceiling, wall and floor enfolding the second floor then runs across to the outer wall on the east side. Finally it extends all the way up to the roof that spans the whole building.

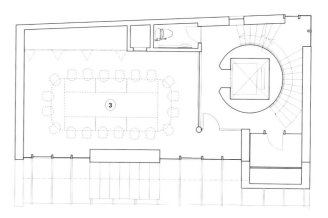

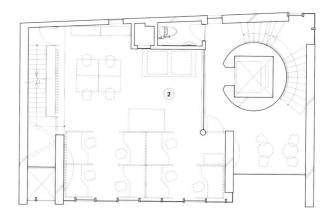

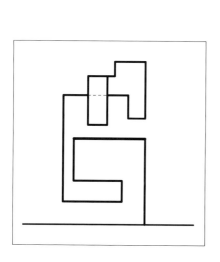

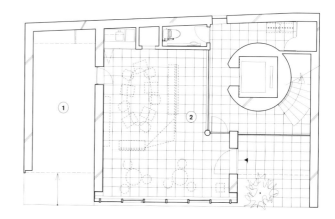

Plans of the sixth, third and first floors.
Key: 1 car park 2 office 3 conference room.
Views of the computer model.

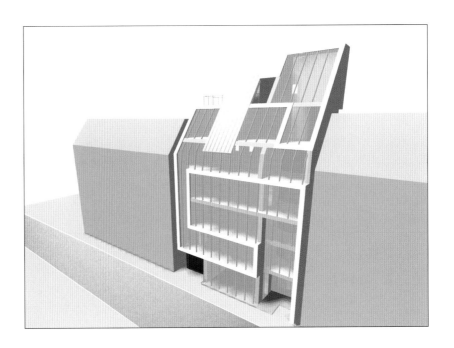

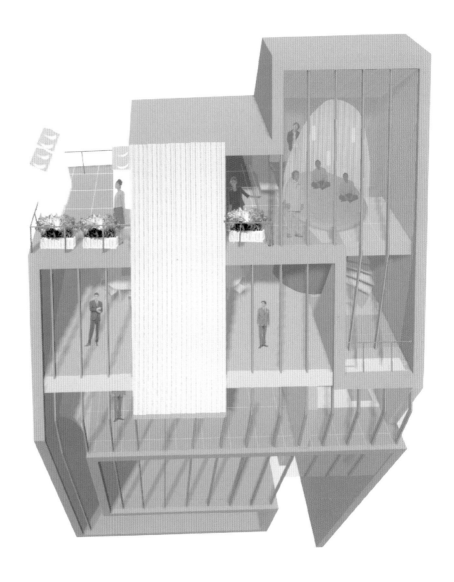

Halftecture T
park with amenities
Maihara-cho, Shiga, 1999–2001

This project involved laying out a park beside a spring that feeds a stream, with the addition of a rest area and parking lot. The spring and stream were left unchanged but a layered fence was added, running the full length of the site. The fence is made of staggered rows of wooden posts that partly screen the approach from the west. By concealing the objective, they generate a sense of depth. The rest area is surrounded on both sides by a board fence two meters high that excludes the outside world, so that the visitor feels drawn to the spring. The architecture both polarizes and symbolizes (by focusing expectation and curiosity on the spring) and abstracts (by concealing the objective).

It uses screens to focus the visual axes symbolically and overlapping steel tubes to interrupt the sightlines, another form of abstraction. All the elements have quite simple functions and the project can be described as "Halftecture," expressing its essential architectural objective of doing without either interior or exterior.

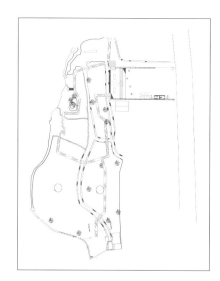

General plan and view of the north front
of the shelter at the park entrance.

West, east, south and north elevations
and plan of the courtyard giving access.
Key: 1 parking lot 2 shelter.
Views of the screened paths inside the park.

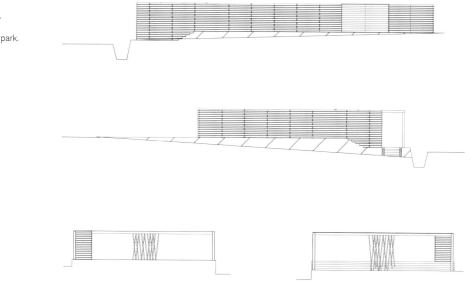

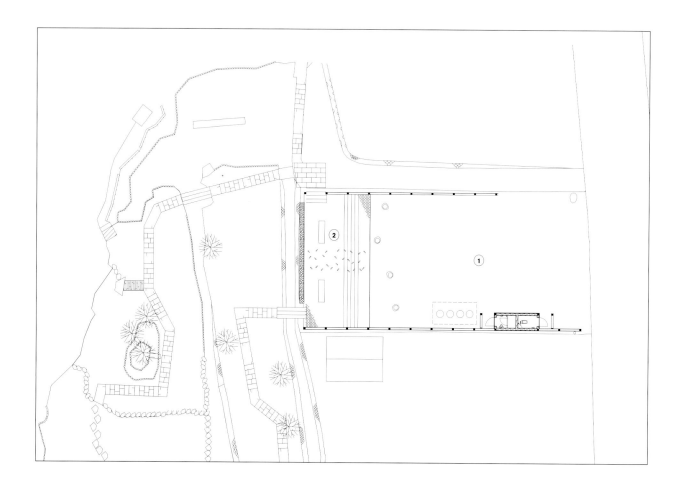

Slowtecture S
cultural center
Maihara-cho, Shiga, 2000-02

The site is a strip of ground lying between a highway and the railroad line. Long and narrow, it stretches 150 meters east to west and 20 meters north to south. It lies on the square in front of the station. To the south runs the historic Nakasendo highway, one of five major roads built in the Edo period, now flanked by a new expressway. The houses of Samegai define a line running east and west; beside them are abundant springs that feed a stream. This site is significant evidence of the way transport technologies have developed over time. The changes are historical evidence of the quest for greater speed.

The exterior of this structure uses weatherproof sheet steel with a standard corrugated surface. It is not a quality material; the goal was not to achieve striking effects by the patches of rust spreading across the surfaces but to reduce loads and simplify work on the building site. It was a practical choice that aimed at economy and ease of maintenance. By the time it was completed, the material had already corroded. This practical fact aroused considerable comment, both favorable and unfavorable. Surface rust forms a stable skin and will not corrode the material beyond a certain point. By deliberately refusing to advertise its strength and durability the structure invites censure or approval.

The building houses two main functions. The first floor has shops run by a local company; the second floor houses a practical training program operated by the town council. Both are intended, as facilities in an important transport junction, to foster the local culture and encourage contacts between locals and outsiders.

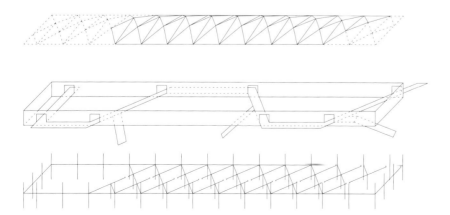

Exploded axonometric projection of structural
components.
View of the south front.

Following pages
Detail of the north front towards the railroad.

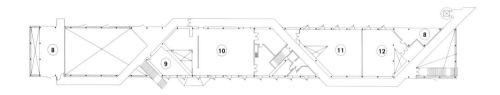

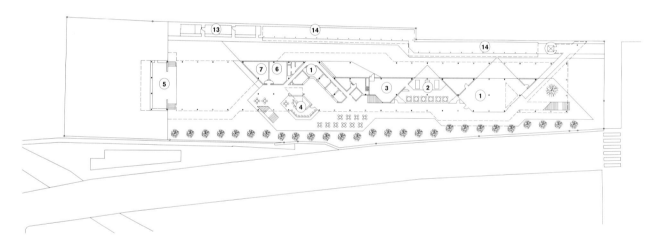

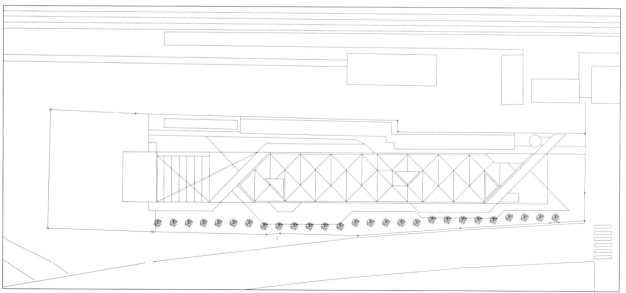

Plans of the second and first floors; general plan.
Key: 1 shop 2 restaurant 3 kitchen 4 cafeteria
5 outdoor stage 6 office 7 waiting room
8 technical plant 9 workshop 10 conference room
11 training room 12 display gallery 13 deposit
14 cycle parking.
The open courtyard at the west end.
View of the outside stairs and the column
of the lift at the east end.

West, east and north sections and elevations.
Detail of the central segment of the south front.

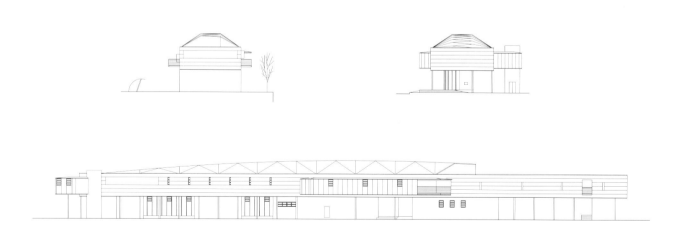

Second-floor conference room.
Details of the corridor traversing the second floor;
the first-floor cafeteria.

Springtecture B
office-home
Biwa-cho, Shiga, 2001-02

This structure is defined by the spiraling progression of a flat continuous surface ("Renzokutai") to form its roof, walls and floors, creating a "Springtecture" of linked discontinuities. While Springtecture Harima progresses by describing a series of arcs, in this structure the design grows out of a combination of arcs and straight lines. It combines an active plane surface with an expanded architectural space. The ramified spaces share their edges (interior/exterior, front/back) to form a productive chain that moves discontinuously from exterior to interior and back to exterior in an architecture of partially shared elements or "Bunyutai."

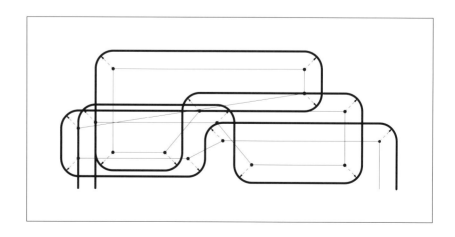

View of the west front.

Views of the computer models and detail
of the dining room in the west end.

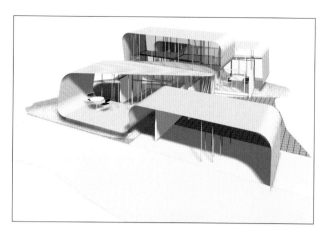

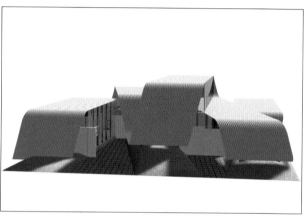

Plan and views of the courtyard on the north front and the urban façade on the east, with the terrace and carport.

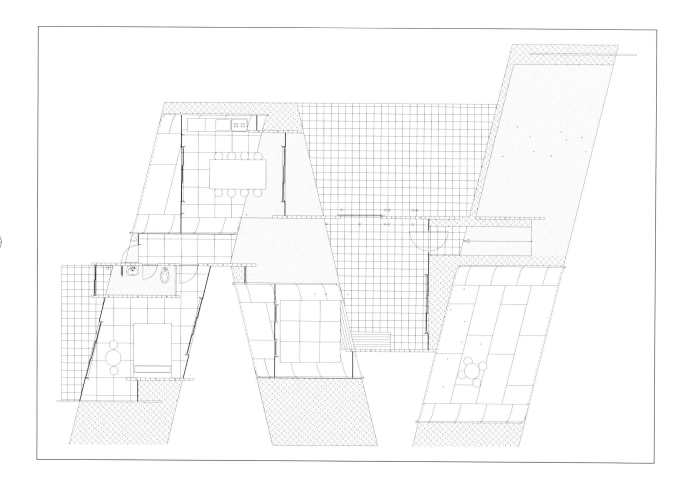

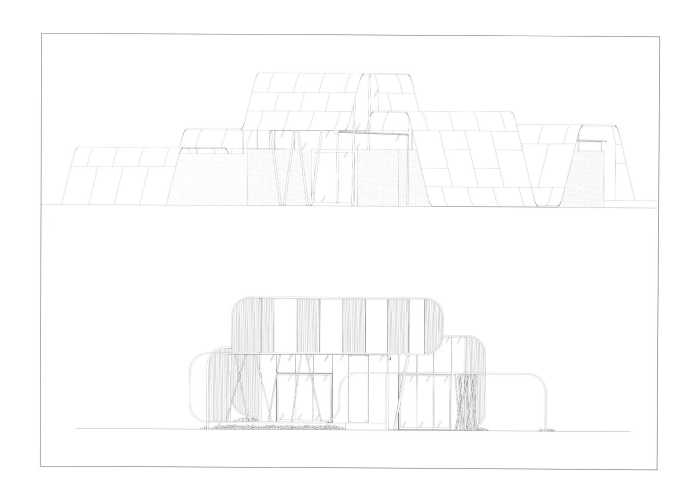

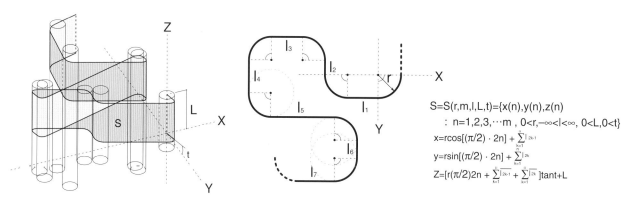

$S=S(r,m,l,L,t)=\{x(n),y(n),z(n)$

$\quad : n=1,2,3,\cdots m \ , \ 0<r,-\infty<l<\infty, \ 0<L,0<t\}$

$x=r\cos[(\pi/2)\cdot 2n]+\sum_{k=1}^{i-1}l_{2k-1}$

$y=r\sin[(\pi/2)\cdot 2n]+\sum_{k=1}^{n}l_{2k}$

$Z=[r(\pi/2)2n+\sum_{k=1}^{i-1}\overline{l_{2k-1}}+\sum_{k=1}^{i}\overline{l_{2k}}]\tan t+L$

North and east elevations and trigonometric
formula for the curvature of the sheet steel.
Detail of the south front.

View of the north front and detail of structural
elements.
View of the central atrium.

appendices

Chronology of Works

The pages numbers of the entries published in this volume
are printed to the right of the photos.

Uenishi House
Higashi Osaka, Osaka-fu
1988

Shinotouseki Nagoya Showroom
Nagoya, Aichi-ken
1989

Architect Last Coating Forum 1990
Chuo-ku, Tokyo-to
1989

Syso Forest
Yamasaki-cho, Hyogo
1989–94

Shinotouseki Car Park
Azai-cho, Shiga-ken
1990
project team: Shinichi Kiyosada (Kiyosada
Structure Office)

Shinotouseki Conference Hall
Azai-cho, Shiga-ken
1990

Third Shinotouseki Azai Factory
Azai-cho, Shiga-ken
1990
project team: Shinichi Kiyosada
(Kiyosada Structure Office)

"Premio internazionale di architettura Andrea
Palladio," 1993

Bibliography: *Nikkei Architecture*, 388, December
1990, pp. 83–87; *Premio internazionale di
architettura Andrea Palladio*, Electa, Milan 1993,
pp. 70–75.

Architect Last Coating Forum 1991
Chiba, Chiba-ken
1991

Tide
Azai-cho, Shiga-ken
1991
project team: Shinichi Kiyosada
(Kiyosada Structure Office)

Bibliography: *Shinkenchiku*, 67, January 1992,
p. 147; *Nikkei Architecture*, 420, January 1992,
p. 167.

Kariguchi City Center Project
Kobe, Hyogo-ken
1992

Project for the Azai Cultural Center
Azai-cho, Shiga-ken
1993

Cyclestation M, bicycle deposit
Maihara-cho, Shiga
1993–94
project team: Shinichi Kiyosada
(Kiyosada Structure Office)

"SD Review Award," 1994
"Commercial Space Design Encouragement Prix,"
1995
"Setsu Watanabe Architectural Prize," 1995
"Architect Grand Prix in Kansai," 1999

Bibliography: *SD*, 363, December 1994,
pp. 10–11; *GA Japan*, 12, January–February 1995,
pp. 194–97; *Shinkenchiku*, 70, February 1995,
pp. 194–97; *SD*, 371, August 1995,
pp. 46–47; *SD*, 400, January 1998,
p. 233; *SD*, 411, December 1998, pp. 93–94,
102–08; *Space*, 376, March 1999, pp. 140–41;
Shuhei Endo, GG Portfolio, Gustavo Gili,
Barcelona 1999, pp. 8–11; *Japan Commercial
Space Design Selection*, "Chinese Architecture
& Industry," 2001, pp. 222–23; *Endo Shuhei
Paramodern*, Amus Arts Press, Osaka 2002.

22

Project for the Kawara Museum
Oumihachiman, Shiga-ken
1993

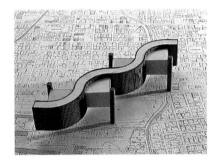

Komachi Project
Oomiya-cho, Kyoto-fu
1994

Transtreet Geba, park and playground
Fukui, Fukui-ken
1994–96
project team: Shinichi Kiyosada (Kiyosada
Structure Office)

"Culture & Architecture in Hokuriku Award," 1996

Bibliography: *Nikkei Architecture*, 567, November
1996, pp. 100–03; *Shinkenchiku*, 71, December
1996, pp. 160–65; *Annual of Space Design
in Japan*, 1997, pp. 268–69.

32

Skintecture I, fish research centre
Shingu-cho, Hyogo-ken
1994–96
project team: Shinichi Kiyosada
(Kiyosada Structure Office)

Grand Prix, "Commercial Space Design," 1997

Bibliography: *Nikkei Architecture*, 570, December 1996, pp. 18–20; *Shinkenchiku*, 72, January 1997, pp. 40–41; *Nikkei Architecture*, 574, February 1997, p. 139; *Annual of Space Design in Japan*, 1997, pp. 18–19; *SD*, 411, December 1998, pp. 93, 96, 102–08; *Shuhei Endo, GG Portfolio*, Gustavo Gili, Barcelona 1999, pp. 16–21; *The Architectural Map of Osaka/Kobe*, Toto, Tokyo 1999, p. 313; *Spazio Architettura*, 47, September 2001, pp. 28, 38–40; *Endo Shuhei Paramodern*, Amus Arts Press, Osaka 2002.

36

Rooftecture Oohashi, house
Nagaokakyo, Kyoto-fu
1995
project team: Aoi Fujioka

Bibliography: *The Architectural Map of Kyoto*, Toto, Tokyo 1998, p. 189.

Fukui Transtreet
Fukui, Fukui-ken
1995
project team: Shinichi Kiyosada
(Kiyosada Structure Office)

Bibliography: *Landscape Design*, 4, Spring 1996, p. 154.

Healtecture K, home-clinic
Takatsuki, Osaka
1994–96
project team: Shinichi Kiyosada (Kyosada Structure Office), Takahito Itiji (Itiji Structure Office)

"Commercial Space Design Encouragement Prix," 1996
"Architect Grand Prix in Kansai," 1999

Bibliography: *GA Japan*, 17, November–December 1995, pp. 64–65; *Shinkenchiku Jyutakutokusyu*, 120, April 1996, pp. 64–71; *Nikkei Architecture*, 599, December 1997, pp. 142–43; *SD*, 411, December 1998, pp. 93, 95, 102–08; *Space*, 376, March 1999, pp. 142–44; *The Architectural Map of Osaka/Kobe*, Toto, Tokyo 1999, p. 141; *Shuhei Endo, GG Portfolio*, Gustavo Gili, Barcelona 1999, pp. 12–15; *Dialogue*, 39, August 2000, pp. 88–93; *Architecti*, 54, 2001, pp. 52–59; *Endo Shuhei Paramodern*, Amus Arts Press, Osaka 2002.

26

Nada House
Kobe, Hyogo-ken
1996

Project for the Saiwai Bridge
Fukui, Fukui-ken
1996

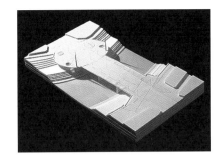

Project for the Ashiya Camping Site
Ashiya, Hyogo-ken
1996

Transtation O, station shelter
Sakai-cho, Fukui
1995–97
project team: Shinichi Kiyosada
(Kiyosada Structure Office)

"SD Review Award," 1995
Grand Prix, "Commercial Space Design," 1997
"Kenneth F. Brown Asia Pacific Culture and
Architecture Award," 1998
"Japan Federation of Architects and Building
Engineers Associations Award," 1998

Bibliography: *SD*, 375, December 1995, pp.
35–37; *Nikkei Architecture*, 571, January 1997,
pp. 130–31; *Shinkenchiku*, 72, January 1997,
pp. 246–50; *The Architectural Review*, April 1997,
pp. 26–27; *Wallpaper*, 6, September–October
1997, p. 40; "Annual of Space Design in Japan,"
1997, pp. 10–11; *SD*, 400, January 1998,
p. 242; *The Architects Journal*, 207, April 1998,
pp. 52–53; *SD*, 411, December 1998, pp. 93, 97,
102–08; *Shuhei Endo, GG Portfolio*, Gustavo Gili,
Barcelona 1999, pp. 22–29; *Dialogue*, 37, June
2000, pp. 90–97; *Detail* (Japan), 2772, June–July,
pp. 629–32; *40 architects under 40*, Taschen,
Cologne 2000, pp. 254–57; *Hinge*, 70, 2000,
pp. 74–75; *ViA arquitectura*, 47, September 2000,
pp. 74–75; *Casabella*, 690, June 2001, pp.
48–49; *Spazio Architettura*, 47, September 2001,
pp. 28, 36–37; *Quaderns*, 231, 2001, pp. 86–91;
High Tech para High Tech, Loft Publications,
Barcelona 2001, pp. 112–19; *Endo Shuhei
Paramodern*, Amus Arts Press, Osaka 2002.

40

Rooftecture I
1997

Bibliography: *40 architects under 40*, 2000;
*Città: Third Millennium International Competition
of Ideas*, La Biennale di Venezia, Actar/Marsilio,
Venice 2001, p. 18; *Spazio Architettura*, 47,
September 2001, p. 36; *High Tech para High
Tech*, Loft Publications, Barcelona 2001, p. 116;
Endo Shuhei Paramodern, Amus Arts Press,
Osaka 2002.

Rooftecture T, square with facilities
Fukui, Fukui-ken
1996–97
project team: Shinichi Kiyosada
(Kiyosada Structure Office)

"View Planning in Fukui Award," 1997

Bibliography: *GA Japan*, 25, March–April 1997, pp. 150–51; *Shinkenchiku*, 72, December 1997, pp. 180–83; *Nikkei Architecture*, 597, November 1997, pp. 112–13; *Marble Architectural Award '98 East Asia*, exhibition catalogue, Internazionale Marmi e Macchine, Carrara 1999, p. 56; *Shuhei Endo, GG Portfolio*, Gustavo Gili, Barcelona 1999, pp. 42–45.

50

Halftecture F, station shelter
Fukui, Fukui-ken
1996–97
project team: Shinichi Kiyosada
(Kiyosada Structure Office)

Grand Prix, "Inter-Intra Space Design Selection," 1997
"The Branch Director's Prix," SDA Design, 1998

Bibliography: *Shinkenchiku*, 73, February 1998, pp. 181–83; *SD*, 411, December 1998, pp. 93, 98–99, 102–08; *Space*, 376, March 1999, pp. 30–33; *Shuhei Endo, GG Portfolio*, Gustavo Gili, Barcelona 1999, pp. 30–33; *Casabella*, 690, June 2001, pp. 50–51; *Endo Shuhei Paramodern*, Amus Arts Press, Osaka 2002.

46

Springtecture H, public toilets
Shingu-cho, Hyogo-ken
1997–98
project team: Norihide Imagawa, Katuhiko Okamoto, Masayoshi Maeda (Tis & Partners)

"Architect Grand Prix in Kansai," 1999
"23rd Hiroba Award," 1999
"Good Design Award," 1999
"AACA Award," 1999
Grand Prix, "ar+d Award," 2000
Finalist, "Premio internazionale di architettura Francesco Borromini," 2001
"8th Public Architecture Award," 2002

Bibliography: *Shinkenchiku*, 73, February 1998, pp. 184–85; *Shinkenchiku*, 23, July 1998, pp. 215–20; *GA Japan*, 33, July–August 1998, pp. 110–13; *The Architectural Review*, 1220, October 1998, pp. 49–51; *Nikkei Architecture*, 627, November 1998, pp. 131–33; *SD*, 411, December 1998, pp. 93, 100–08; *Sci-Fi Architecture*, 69, March–April 1999, pp. 86–89; *L'Architecture d'aujourd'hui*, 325, December 1999, pp. 70–71; *Shuhei Endo, GG Portfolio*, Gustavo Gili, Barcelona 1999, pp. 34–41; *The Architectural Map of Osaka/Kobe*, Toto, Tokyo 1999, p. 336; *Archilab Orléans 2000*, exhibition catalogue, Orléans, 2000, pp. 218–21; *de Architect*, April 2000, pp. 20–21; *L'Oeil*, 516, May 2000, p. 12; *Dialogue*, 37, June 2000, pp. 98–105; *ViA arquitectura*, November 2000, pp. 88–91; *Ca M'interesse*, 237, November 2000, p. 164; *Nikkei Architecture*, 680, November 2000, p. 15; *Structure as Design*, Rockport Publisher, Massachusetts 2000, pp. 80–85; *Hinge*, 70, 2000, p. 75; *Hauser*, February 2001, p. 14; *Wallpaper*, 37, April 2001, p. 50; *Monument*, 41, April–May 2001, p. 59; *Ish*, 177, August 2001, pp. 102–05; *Spazio Architettura*, September 2001, pp. 28–31; *Wallpaper*, September 2001, pp. 126–31; *Interni, il magazine del design*, special issue accompanying *Panorama*, 13, October 2001, pp. 19–20; *Architectural Record*, December 2001, pp. 60–61; *Detail* (Japan), 149, summer 2001, pp. 50–51; *Hinge*, 73, 2001, p. 31; *Casabella*, 690, June 2001, pp. 44–47; *Casabella*, 691, July–August 2001, p. 78; *XS: Big Ideas, Small Buildings*, Thames and Hudson, London 2001, pp. 132–135; P. Gossel, *Architecture in the Twentieth Century*, Taschen, Cologne 2001, p. 401; *New trends of architecture in Europe and Japan 2001*, international exhibition catalogue, Shinkenchiku-sha, Tokyo 2001, pp. 78–81; *Bauwelt*, 93, February 2002, pp. 28–29; *Diseño Interior*, 114, 2002, pp. 74–76; *Endo Shuhei Paramodern*, Amus Arts Press, Osaka 2002; *Ottagono*, 152, July–August 2002, pp. 62–64.

56

Rooftecture O, cultural center
Shimizu-cho, Fukui
1996–98
project team: Shinichi Kiyosada
(Kiyosada Structure Office)

"Lighting Diffusion Award," 1998
First prize ex-aequo in section 2 of the "Marble
Architectural Award, East Asia," 1999
Award for Excellence, "Practical Use of Wood
Contest," 1999

Bibliography: *Marble Architectural Award '98
East Asia*, exhibition catalogue, Internazionale
Marmi e Macchine, Carrara 1999, pp. 26–31;
Shinkenchiku, 74, March 1999, pp. 185–90;
Shuhei Endo, GG Portfolio, Gustavo Gili,
Barcelona 1999, pp. 52–57; *40 architects
under 40*, Taschen, Cologne 2000, pp. 240–47.

74

Rooftecture H, office building
Himeji, Hyogo-ken
1996–98
project team: Masashi Ouji (Design-Structure
Institute)

"View Planning in Himeji City Award," 2000

Bibliography: *The Architectural Map of
Osaka/Kobe*, Toto, Tokyo 1999, p. 319.

80

**Rooftecture N, office block and deposit
for building materials**
Nishinomiya, Hyogo-ken
1997–98
project team: Masashi Ouji (Design-Structure
Institute)

Grand Prix, "Commercial Space Design," 1997
"1st Isoband Isodahha Design Contest," 1998

Bibliography: *Architectural Design*, 69,
March–April 1999, pp. 86–89; *The Architectural
Map of Osaka/Kobe*, Toto, Tokyo 1999, p. 216;
Shuhei Endo, GG Portfolio, Gustavo Gili,
Barcelona 1999, pp. 46–51.

66

Transtreet Togo
Fukui, Fukui-ken
1998

"View Planning in Fukui Award," 1997
"Marble Architectural Award, East Asia," 1999

Bibliography: *Zoukei*, 31, February 2001,
pp. 66–67; *Dialogue*, 36, May 2000,
pp. 100–03; *Marble Architectural Award '98
East Asia*, exhibition catalogue, Internazionale
Marmi e Macchine, Carrara 1999, pp. 56–57.

Project for the Kohoku Cultural Center
Kohoku-cho, Shiga-ken
1998

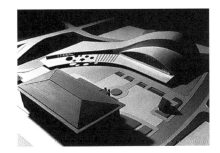

Renzokutai Chair
1998

Project for the Biwa Kindergarten
Biwa-cho, Shiga-ken
1998

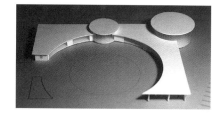

Rooftecture Y, health spa
Yamasaki-cho, Hyogo-ken
1997–98
project team: Shinichi Kiyosada
(Kiyosada Structure Office)

Bibliography: *Kenchikubunka*, 640, February 2000, pp. 32–40; *40 architects under 40*, Taschen, Cologne 2000, pp. 248–53; *Hinge*, 70, 2000, p. 76; *Dialogue*, 47, May 2001, pp. 122–27; *Spazio Architettura*, 47, November 2001, pp. 28, 41–42.

88

Samegai Cyclestation, bicycle shelter
Maihara-cho, Shiga-ken
1998–99
project team: Shinichi Kiyosada
(Kiyosada Structure Office)

Project for the Matsuoka Sport Center
Matsuoka-cho, Fukui-ken
1999

**Springtecture NHK, competition project
for an ecological house**
Inagi, Tokyo-to
1999

100

Door Handle
1999

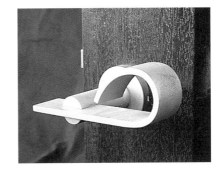

Rooftecture B, farm emporium
Biwa-cho, Shiga-ken
1998–2000
project team: Norihide Imagawa, Katsuhiko
Okamoto (Tis & Partners)

Bibliography: *Shinkenchiku*, 75, August 2000,
pp. 174–77; *Architectural Record*, December
2001, p. 62; *Endo Shuhei Paramodern*,
Amus Arts Press, Osaka 2002.

112

Rooftecture A, apartment block
Taitou-ku, Tokyo
1998–2000
project team: Norihide Imagawa, Kiyofumi Murano
(Tis & Partners)

"2nd Isoband Isodahha Design Contest," 2001

Bibliography: *GA Houses*, 59, December 1999,
pp. 54–55; *30 House Plots by 30 architects in
their 30's*, exhibition catalogue, Gap, Tokyo 2000,
pp. 36–39.

118

Rooftecture K, office building
Nishinomiya, Hyogo-ken
1998–2000
project team: Shinichi Kiyosada (Kiyosada
Structure Office)

Bibliography: *L'Architecture d'aujourd'hui*, 329,
July–August 2000, pp. 36–37; *Shinkenchiku*,
75, August 2000, pp. 178–83; *Hinge*,
September–October 2000, p. 76; *Ish*, 177,
August 2001, pp. 102–05; *Spazio Architettura*,
47, September 2001, pp. 28, 32–35; *Detail*
(Japan), 147, summer 2001, pp. 58–60;
Architectural Record, December 2001, p. 62;
Endo Shuhei Paramodern, Amus Arts Press,
Osaka 2002.

106

Rooftecture II
2000

Bibliography: *Shinkenchiku*, 75, August 2000, p. 183; *Endo Shuhei Paramodern*, Amus Arts Press, Osaka 2002.

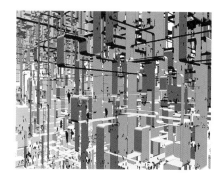

Springtecture A, competition project for an art museum
Aomori, Aomori-ken
1999–2000

Bibliography: *Archilab Orléans 2000*, exhibition catalogue, Orléans 2000, pp. 222–23; *Monument*, 41, April–May 2001, p. 59; *Architectural Record*, December 2001, p. 63; *Ottagono*, 152, July–August 2002, p. 65; *Endo Shuhei Paramodern*, Amus Arts Press, Osaka 2002.

96

Springtecture I
2000

First prize "Third Millennium International Competition of Ideas," 7th Venice Architecture Biennale, 1999

Bibliography: *Città: Third Millennium International Competition of Ideas*, Venice Biennale, Actar/Marsilio, Venice 2001, pp. 16–19; AA.VV, *Archilab Orléans 2000*, 2000, p. 222; *5° Festival di architettura in video "Il futuro e la città,"* exhibition catalogue, Department of Architecture, Università degli studi di Firenze, Florence 2000, p. 52; *Architectural Record*, December 2001, p. 63; *New trends of architecture in Europe and Japan 2001*, international exhibition catalogue, Shinkenchiku-sha, Tokyo 2001, p. 79; *Endo Shuhei Paramodern*, Amus Arts Press, Osaka 2002.

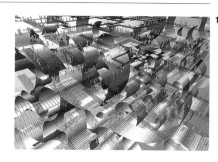

104

Rooftecture WIPO, competition project
Geneva, Switzerland
1999–2000

Finalist, "WIPO International Competition," 2000

Bibliography: *Archilab Orléans 2000*, exhibition catalogue, Orléans 2000, pp. 224–25; *Architectural Record*, December 2001, p. 62.

126

Springtecture Orléans, temporary installation
Orléans, France
1999–2000
project team: Shinichi Kiyosada
(Kiyosada Structure Office)

"Public Architecture Award," 2000

Bibliography: *Endo Shuhei Paramodern*, Amus Arts Press, Osaka 2002.

130

Rooftecture Wave, canopy for a used-car lot
Minou, Osaka–fu
2000–01
project team: Shinichi Kiyosada
(Kiyosada Structure Office)

Bibliography: *Endo Shuhei Paramodern*,
Amus Arts Press, Osaka 2002.

136

Transtreet Hikida
Hikida, Fukui-ken
2000–01

**Springtecture S, competition project
for a ferry terminal**
Sasebo, Nagasaki-ken
2000–01

Bibliography: *Ish*, 177, August 2001, pp. 102–05;
*New trends of architecture in Europe
and Japan 2001*, international exhibition catalogue,
Shinkenchiku-sha, Tokyo 2001, pp. 78–81; *Endo
Shuhei Paramodern*, Amus Arts Press, Osaka
2002.

132

Rooftecture U, office block
Oku-cho, Okayama-ken
1999–2001
project team: Shinichi Kiyosada
(Kiyosada Structure Office)

140

Rooftecture U, factory
Oku-cho, Okayama-ken
1999–2001
project team: Shinichi Kiyosada
(Kiyosada Structure Office)

140

Rooftecture Gifu Project
Hagiwara-cho, Gifu-ken
2001

Rooftecture M, office-home
Maruoka-cho, Fukui-ken
2000–01
project team: Masashi Ouji
(Design-Structure Institute)

Bibliography: *Archilab Orléans 2001*, Orléans
2001, pp. 108–09; *Mohntop*, 5, 2001, pp. 46–48;
Nueuos concepts de vivienda, Loft Publications,
Barcelona 2001, pp. 150–55; *Casabella*, 702,
July–August 2002, pp. 14–21.

146

Halftecture T, park with amenities
Maihara-cho, Shiga-ken
1999–2001
project team: Shinichi Kiyosada
(Kiyosada Structure Office)

Bibliography: *Shinkenchiku*, 77, August 2002,
pp. 135–39.

164

Halftecture Ibotorisui
Maihara-cho, Shiga-ken
1999–2001
project team: Shinichi Kiyosada
(Kiyosada Structure Office)

Halftecture Saigyousui
Maihara-cho, Shiga-ken
1999–2001

Rooftecture Rome, project for a residential complex
Rome, Italy
2001

Bubbletecture Aomori Project
Aomori, Aomori-ken
2001

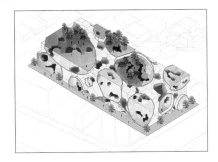

Bubbletecture Singapore Project
Singapore
2001

Obama Complex Project
Obama, Fukui-ken
2001

Samegai Pumping Station
Maihara-cho, Shiga-ken
2001

JR Samegai Station, study rendering
Maihara-cho, Shiga-ken
2001

Slowtecture S, cultural center
Maihara-cho, Shiga-ken
2000–02
project team: Norihide Imagawa, Yuji Hatano
(Tis & Partners)

Bibliography: *GA Japan*, 56, May–June 2002,
pp. 48–59.

168

Rooftecture C, crematorium
Taishi-cho, Hyogo-ken
2000–
project team: Norihide Imagawa, Takeshi Fukunaga
(Tis & Partners)

154

**Apartment Osaka,
apartment complex**
Katano, Osaka-fu
2000–
project team: Norihide Imagawa, Yuji Hatano
(Tis & Partners)

158

Salzburg Springtecture Project
Salzburg, Austria
2001

Springtecture B, office-home
Biwa-cho, Shiga-ken
2001–02
project team: Norihide Imagawa, Yuji Hatano
(Tis & Partners)

178

Rooftecture S, office building
Osaka, Osaka-fu
2001–
project team: Shinichi Kiyosada
(Kiyosada Structure Office)

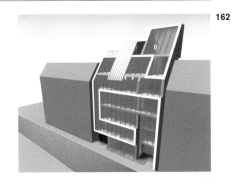

162

Bubbletecture M, kindergarten
Maihara-cho, Shiga-ken
2001–
project team: Mitsuhiro Kanada, Ryota Kidokoro
(Ove Arup & Partners Japan Ltd.)

160

**Shanghai Talun Road, project
for "The City of Men of Culture"**
Shanghai, China
2001–02

Springtecture Project, Egypt
Giza, Egypt
2002

Biography

1960

Born in Shiga Prefecture, Japan.

1986

Obtained a master's degree
from the Kyoto City University of Art.

1986–88

Joins Osamu Ishii & Biken
Associates.

1988

Founded Shuhei Endo Architect
Institute.

Teaching Posts

1988–94

Fukui College of Technology.

1994–99

Kyoto Junior College of Art and
Design.

1997–2001

Kobe Design University.

1997–2002

Kinki University.

1998–2002

Kyoto University of Art and Design.

2001–02

Kobe University.

2001–02

Kyoto City University of Art.

Juries

1997

43rd Osaka Architecture Contest.

1999

45th Osaka Architecture Contest.

2002

Japan Culture Design Contest (JIDF).

Awards

1993

"Premio Internazionale d'architettura
Andrea Palladio" for the third
Shinotouseki Azai factory.

1994

"SD Review Award" for Cyclestation
M.

1995

"SD Review Award" for Transtation O.

"Commercial Space Design
Encouragement Prix"
for Cyclestation M.

"Setsu Watanabe Architectural Prize"
for Cyclestation M.

1996

"Culture & Architecture in
Hokuriku Award" for Transtreet G.

"Commercial Space Design
Encouragement Prix"
for Healtecture K.

1997

Grand Prix, "Commercial Space
Design" for Transtation O.

"Commercial Space Design
Encouragement Prix"
for Skintecture I.

"Commercial Space Design
Encouragement Prix"
for Rooftecture N.

"View Planning in Fukui Award"
for Rooftecture T.

"View Planning in Fukui Award"
for Transtreet T.

Grand Prix, "Inter-Intra Space Design
Selection," for Halftecture F.

1998

"Kenneth F. Brown Asia Pacific
Culture and Architecture Award"
for Transtation O.

"Japan Federation of Architects
and Building Engineers Associations
Award" for Transtation O.

"SDA Design Award," "The Branch
Director's Prize" for Halftecture F.

"Lighting Diffusion Award"
for Rooftecture O.

"1st Isoband Isodahha Design
Contest" for Rooftecture N.

1999

"Architect Grand Prix in Kansai"
for Cyclestation M, Healtecture K
and Springtecture H.

"23rd Hiroba Award" for
Springtecture H.

Award for Excellence, "Practical Use
of Wood Contest" for Rooftecture O.

"Good Design Award" for
Springtecture H.

"AACA Award" for Springtecture H.

First Prize ex-aequo for the
2nd section of the "Marble
Architectural Award, East Asia"
for Rooftecture O.

"Marble Architectural Award,
East Asia" for Transtreet T.

First prize, "Third Millennium
International Competition
of Ideas," 7th Venice Architecture
Biennale for Springtecture I.

2000

Grand Prix, "ar+d Award" for
Springtecture H.

"View Planning in Himeji City
Award" for Rooftecture H.

Finalist, "WIPO International
Competition" with Rooftecture.

2001

Finalist, "Premio internazionale
di architettura Francesco Borromini"
with Springtecture H.

"2nd Isoband Isodahha Design
Contest" for Rooftecture A.

2002

"8th Public Architecture Award"
for Springtecture H.

Exhibitions

1992

"100 Modern Architects," 3rd edition,
Kumamoto, Tokyo.

1993

"100 Modern Architects," 4th edition,
Tokyo.

"Premio Internazionale d'architettura
Andrea Palladio," 4th edition, Venice,
Italy.

"Architect Andepandan," 1st edition
Kyoto.

1994

"SD Review," 13th edition, Tokyo,
Osaka.

1995

"SD Review," 14th edition, Tokyo.

"GA Japan League," Tokyo.

"Tower Art in Tsutenkaku," Osaka.

1996

"The Photograph Exhibition for the
Revival in the Brewing Town," Kobe.

"Architect Andepandan," 2nd edition,
Kyoto.

1997

"GA House Project," Tokyo.

"The Possibility of Architecture –
House Exhibition," Osaka.

1998

"The Possibility of Architecture –
Project 1999," Osaka.

1999

"Architect Grand Prix in Kansai,"
Osaka.

"GA House," Tokyo.

"Marble Architectural Awards, East
Asia and Europe," Carrara, Italy.

2000

"ArchiLab Orléans 2000," Orléans,
France.

7th Venice Architecture Biennale,
Venice, Italy.

"30 House Plots by 30 architects
in their 30's," Tokyo.

"10 City Profiles from 10 Young
Architects," Tokyo.

"Il futuro e la città," 5th International
festival of architecture in video,
Florence, Italy.

"New Trends of Architecture
in Europe and Japan 2001," Japan,
Portugal, The Netherlands.

2001

"ArchiLab Orléans 2001," Orléans,
France.

2002

"45 under 45," Vienna, Austria.

2003

Exhibition in Bellinzona, Switzerland.

Bibliography

Writings by Shuhei Endo

1992

"Tide," in *Shinkenchiku*, January,
p. 147.

1993

*Premio internazionale di architettura
Andrea Palladio*, Electa, Milan 1993,
pp. 70–75.

1994

"From town of Renaissance,"
in *Shinkenchiku*, January, p. 113.

"To Deceleration from Acceleration,"
in *SD*, 363, December, p. 11;
republished in *GA Japan*, 12,
January–February 1995, p. 196;
in *Shinkenchiku*, February 1995,
p. 197; in *SD*, 371, August 1995,
p. 46; in *Space*, 376, March 1999,
p. 140.

1995

"To communication from encounter,
To contact consequently,"
in *Kenchikubunka*, 50, October,
pp. 4–5.

"Smooth Flow," in *GA Japan*,
17, November–December, p. 64.

"To stop from Deceleration," in *SD*,
375, December, p. 37; republished in
Dialogue, 37, June 2000,
pp. 92, 95; in *Detail*, June–July
2000, p. 630; in *ViA arquitectura*,
vol. VIII, February 2000, pp. 84–85.

1996

"Monthly comment for Shinkenchiku,"
in *Shinkenchiku*, monthly.

"Landscape formulated by slow
down," in *Landscape Design*, 3,
p. 154.

"Opening by means of membrane,"
in *Shinkenchiku Jyutakutokusyu*,
April, pp. 70–71; republished in
Space, 376, March 1999,
pp. 142, 144; republished in
Dialogue, 39, August 2000,
pp. 91–92; in *Architecti*, 54,
April–May–July 2001, pp. 52–53.

"Belt of Discontinuty to regulate,
the speed," in *Shinkenchiku*,
December, pp. 164–65.

1997

"Side of Discontinuty," in
Shinkenchiku, January, p. 245.

"Be Scattered," in *GA Japan*, 25,
March–April, p. 150.

"Belt of Discontinuty,"
in *Shinkenchiku*, December, p. 183.

1998

"A Half Architecture,"
in *Shinkenchiku*, February, p. 183;
republished in *Space*, 376, March
1999, p. 138.

"Possibility that holding a part
in common," in *Shinkenchiku*, 73,
February, p. 185, and July, p. 219;
republished in *GA Japan*, 33,
July–August, pp. 112–13;
in *Space*, 376, March 1999,
pp. 134–36; in *ViA arquitectura*,
vol. VIII, February 2000, p. 88;
in *Dialogue*, 37, June 2000,
pp. 98–101; in *New trends of*

*architecture in Europe and Japan
2001*, international exhibition
catalogue, Shinkenchiku-sha, Tokyo
2001, p. 79.

"Halftecture Project," in *SD*, 411,
December, p. 93.

Basic design, University of Art
and Design, Kyoto.

The Architectural Map of Kyoto, Toto,
Tokyo.

1999

"Partial Intervention,"
in *Shinkenchiku*, March, p.190.

"Silence of the end of Millenniums,"
in *SD*, 423, December, p. 59.

"Winding and Repetition of
Connective," in *GA Houses*, 59,
p. 55.

*The Architectural Map of
Osaka/Kobe*, Toto, Tokyo.

"Rooftecture O," in *Marble
Architectural Award '98 East Asia*,
exhibition catalogue, Internazionale
Marmi e Macchine, Carrara, p. 30.

"Shuhei Endo," *GG Portfolio*,
Gustavo Gili, Barcelona.

2000

"Strip of Continuity,"
in *Kenchikubunka*, 640, February,
p. 37; republished in *Dialogue*, 47,
May 2001, pp. 123, 126.

"Flowing with the history,"
in *Dialogue*, 36, May,
pp. 100–02.

"Paramodern Architecture," in
Archilab Orléans 2000, exhibition
catalogue edited by M.-A. Brayer and
F. Migayrou, Orléans, p. 218;
republished in *New trends
of architecture in Europe and Japan
2001*, international exhibition
catalogue, Shinkenchiku-sha, Tokyo
2001, p. 78.

*30 House Plots by 30 architects
in their 30's*, exhibition catalogue,
Gap, Tokyo, pp. 36–39.

2001

"Rooftecture M," in *Nueuos concepts
de vivienda*, Loft Publications,
Barcelona, p. 152.

"Springtecture S," in *New trends of
architecture in Europe and Japan
2001*, international exhibition
catalogue, Shinkenchiku-sha, Tokyo,
p. 79.

*Città: Third Millennium International
Competition of Ideas*, La Biennale
di Venezia, Actar/Marsilio, Venice,
pp. 16–19.

*10 City Profiles from 10 Young
Architects*, exhibition catalogue, Toto,
Tokyo.

2002

"Weak Architecture," in *GA Japan*,
56, May–June, pp. 50–51.

"Hide and Concentration," in
Shinkenchiku, 77, August, p. 139.

Endo Shuhei Paramodern, Amus
Arts Press, Osaka.

Writings on Shuhei Endo

1997

V. Pease, "Making waves,"
in *The Architectural Review*, 1202,
April, pp. 26–27.

E. O'Kelly, "Shining example,"
in *Wallpaper*, 6,
September–October, p. 40.

1998

N. McLaughlin, "Building favourites,"
in *The Architects Journal*, 207, April,
pp. 52–53.

P. McGuire, "Metal Turnings,"
in *The Architectural Review*, 1220,
October, pp. 49–50.

K. Matsuba, "Visionary Modernism
of the end of the 20th century,"
in *SD*, 411, December, pp. 106–07.

1999

M. Toy, "Rooftecture e Facility for a
park," in *Sci-Fi Architecture*, p. 87.

K. Nute, "Folded, curved, and twisted
space: Shuhei Endo and the
architecture of the convoluted live,"
in *Shuhei Endo, GG Portfolio*,
Gustavo Gili, Barcelona, pp. 4–7.

2000

D. Caramma, "In the nature
of materials," in *Spazio Architettura*,
47, April, p. 28.

"Global perspective," in *Hinge*, 70,
pp. 74–76. N. Jankovic, "The success
of MigayrouLab," in *L'Oeil*, 516, May,
p. 12.

S. Trelcat, "Rooftecture K, Office
Building," *L'Architecture
d'aujourd'hui*, 329, July–August,
p. 36.

K. Nute, "Shuhei Endo," in *10+1*, 22,
pp. 154–57.

S. Allaire, P. Chabard, "Springtecture
H, Springtecture A, Rooftecture W,"
in *Archilab Orléans 2000*, exhibition
catalogue edited by M.-A. Brayer
and F. Migayrou, Orléans, pp. 219,
222, 224.

I. Allen, "Park keeper's apartment
and park lavatories," in *Structure as
Design*, Rockport Publishers,
Massachusetts, p. 80.

J. Cargill Thompson, "Shuhei Endo,"
in *40 architects under 40*, Taschen,
Cologne, p. 241.

J. Cargill Thompson, "Rooftecture O,"
in *40 architects under 40*, Taschen,
Cologne, p. 242.

2001

D. Roderick, "Hot tin roof," in
Wallpaper, April, p. 50.

C. Baglione, "Shuhei Endo," in
Casabella, 690, June, p. 44.

C. Low, "Gyoza, Zen and
Architecture," in *Ish*, 177, August,
p. 102.

P. Richardson, "Going with the flow,"
in *The World of Interiors*, September,
p. 130.

N.R. Pollock, "Coils and curves
corrugated steel, seamlessly weaving
indoors and out," in *Architectural
Record*, December, p. 60.

G. Thomson, "Transtation O,"
in *Quaderns*, 231, p. 86.

P. Chabard, "Rooftecture M," in
Archilab Orléans 2001, exhibition
catalogue edited by M.-A. Brayer
and F. Migayrou, Orléans,
pp. 108–09.

A. Cuito, L. Gomez, C. Montes,
"Transtation O," in *High Tech para
High Tech*, Loft Publications,
Barcelona, p. 112.

P. Gossel, *Architecture
in the Twentieth Century*, Taschen,
Cologne, p. 401.

P. Richardson, "Curving linear and
New Waves," in *XS: Big Ideas, Small
Buildings*, Thames and Hudson,
London, pp. 98–99, 132–33.

2002

"Casa e atelier Rooftecture M,"
Casabella, 702, July–August 2002,
pp. 14–21.

H. Kashiwagi, "Metal light enough
to float: the architecture of Shuhei
Endo," in *Endo Shuhei Paramodern*,
Amus Arts Press, Osaka, n. p.

E. Gandolfi, "Shuhei Endo: la
superficie domata," in *Ottagono*, 152,
July–August 2002, pp. 62–65.

Collaborators

Aoi Fujioka
Wataru Horie
Atsuo Miyatake
Keisuke Fukuma
Kengo Sasamoto
Naohiro Kobayashi
Takashi Nabeshima

Former Collaborators

Toshinori Nagai
Tetsuya Fukuda
Aya Nakano
Takamitsu Anahara

Photograph Credits

We wish to thank the Shuhei Endo
Architect Institute for having provided
the photographic material published
in this volume.

The photographs published herein
are by:
Yukio Futagawa: p. 10 right
Toshiharu Kitajima: pp. 18, 41, 43,
45, 119, 121, 122–23, 125, 179,
181, 183, 185, 186, 187
Yoshiharu Matsumura: pp. 16
a sinistra, 23, 25, 27, 29, 30, 31, 33,
35, 37, 39, 47, 49, 51, 53, 55, 57,
59, 61, 63, 65, 67, 69, 71, 73, 75,
77, 79, 81, 83, 85, 87, 89, 91,
92–93, 95, 107, 109, 110, 111,
113, 115, 117, 137, 139, 141, 143,
145, 147, 149, 151, 153, 165, 167,
169, 170–171, 173, 175, 176, 177
Junichi Shinomura: p. 10 left
Kei Sugino: pp. 97, 99

Optimization of the drawings is
by Federico Ferme.

Holders of rights to any unidentified
photograph sources should contact
the publisher.